WEB SERVICE
APIs
AND LIBRARIES

WEB SERVICE
APIs
AND LIBRARIES

JASON PAUL MICHEL

An imprint of the American Library Association

Chicago   2013

Jason Paul Michel is user experience librarian at the Miami University Libraries in Oxford, Ohio. He has engineered numerous API projects at the Miami University Libraries, including Vimeo, Flickr, and Twitter API projects, and has presented on these projects at state and national library conferences.

© 2013 by the American Library Association. Any claim of copyright is subject to applicable limitations and exceptions, such as rights of fair use and library copying pursuant to Sections 107 and 108 of the U.S. Copyright Act. No copyright is claimed for content in the public domain, such as works of the U.S. government.

Printed in the United States of America

17 16 15 14 13   5 4 3 2 1

Extensive effort has gone into ensuring the reliability of the information in this book; however, the publisher makes no warranty, express or implied, with respect to the material contained herein.

ISBNs: 978-0-8389-1182-2 (paper); 978-0-8389-9641-6 (PDF). For more information on digital formats, visit the ALA Store at alastore.ala.org and select eEditions.

Library of Congress Cataloging-in-Publication Data
Michel, Jason Paul.
  Web service APIs and libraries / Jason Paul Michel.
      pages   cm.
  Includes index.
  ISBN 978-0-8389-1182-2 (alk. paper)
  1. Web services—Library applications. 2. Application program interfaces (Computer software)
3. Library websites—Design. I. Title.
  Z674.75.W67M53 2013
  025.042'2—dc23

                                                                    2012019725

Cover design by Kim Thornton. Composition in Alegreya and Gotham by Casey Bayer.
Cover image © majcot/Shutterstock, Inc.

⊚ This paper meets the requirements of ANSI/NISO Z39.48-1992 (Permanence of Paper).

CONTENTS

First, I would like to wholeheartedly thank Christopher Rhodes, editor at ALA Editions. His guidance throughout the work was invaluable. Additionally, I'd like to thank my copy editor, Russell Harper, who transformed my haphazard text into effective prose.

The inspiration for this book came from the projects I pursued at the Miami University Libraries. I must thank Elias Tzoc, with whom I worked on a Flickr API project, the success of which led to further API explorations. I also must thank Rob Casson, whose unparalleled programming expertise is matched only by his willingness to lend a hand.

This book would never have been written if not for the encouraging environment at the Miami University Libraries, as led by Dean Judith Sessions. I also would like to thank the gentle prodding of Assistant Deans Lisa Santucci and Aaron Shrimplin.

Finally, I'd like to thank my wonderful wife, Kristi LaFary. She's the inspiration for everything I do and without whom this book would never have been completed, since as Robert Frost wrote, we are "together wing to wing and oar to oar."

Libraries have lost the battle. The web is now, and has been for a while, where people go to find information.

But that is a vague statement. Imagine the web as a huge, vast cityscape. Most of this city consists of sparsely populated back alleys and warrens, while standing at the center are a few heavily populated monoliths: Google, Wikipedia, Facebook, Twitter, IMDb, Flickr, and a few others. These are the places people go to find information.

Our library websites, including our unique digital collections, are found in one of those back alleys, twenty blocks from Google (twenty pages deep). Unfindable. Dusty. Lonely. All is not lost, however. There is a way to put library websites front and center, and that is through the use of APIs. APIs allow programmers and developers to both deliver content to and receive content from the web's larger, more highly used services. At the same time, APIs give developers the tools and data to create valuable, user-friendly services of their own.

So, what type of library services can be developed through the use of APIs? Let's consider some potential applications.

Twitter

The Twitter API can be utilized to programmatically mine tweets coming from users in your area. You can query this data to see if people are tweeting about your institution, or tweeting about reading, books, doing research, and the like. This insight can give you an opportunity for proactive reference or outreach services.

You could also use the Twitter API as an in-house outage reporting tool. This will be discussed in full detail in the chapter on the Twitter API.

Flickr

The Flickr API can be used in many ways. Imagine you have a large collection of interesting digital images that are hosted on your library's website. The audience for these images is limited if they remain only on your site. Using the Flickr API, you can upload large numbers of digital images and accompanying data in a short amount of time. Sharing these images on Flickr will expose your content to a much wider audience.

You can also use the Flickr API to pull images onto your site. For example, you might use it to serve up Flickr content alongside library content related to a current event. Imagine a web page with a dynamic list of library books and articles related to the 2012 presidential election with a slideshow near the top of the page of Flickr images from the campaign trail.

Vimeo

Sometimes you can use a web service API as a means to deliver your own content to your own site, rather than building up unnecessary infrastructure. Vimeo is a prime example of that. Let's say you have instructional videos for your library. Rather than worrying about how to upload a video to your own server, it may be easier to upload your video content to a site like Vimeo and display those videos on your site using their API. We will go through this process in the chapter on Vimeo's API.

Google Charts

Using the Google Charts API, you can add data visualization aspects to your site. The API could be utilized to display in a graphical way how many computers are available in your computer lab, how many laptops or other pieces of circulating equipment are available for checkout, circulation stats, and more.

Bibliographic Service APIs

Utilizing the APIs of web services such as OCLC, LibraryThing, Open Library, Google Books, and others allows you to develop services that can enrich your library catalog: book covers, book reviews, recommendations, full-text e-books, and more.

I. INTENDED AUDIENCE

This book is intended first of all for library school students. Anyone studying library science today must plan on coming away with a good understanding of web technologies to have any hope of shaping our profession and keeping pace with technology. We, as a profession, will be left in the dust if younger librarians don't understand and embrace these technologies.

It is also intended for librarians and library administrators interested in learning how to better integrate their services into the wider web ecosystem. This, I believe, is a critical mission if libraries are to maintain their relevance.

With respect to technical knowledge, the examples in this book are geared toward people with rudimentary knowledge of HTML, PHP, and HTTP. Complete beginners will be able to learn as they go, however, as long as they follow the examples to the letter.

II. WHAT IS AN API?

An API, or application programming interface, is a set of methods to access data in otherwise closed systems. APIs give programmers and developers the tools necessary to build software and services with data and services from external sources. Extending a metaphor used by David Orenstein,[1] let's imagine that you are building a deck in your backyard and you realize that you don't have a hammer. You have three neighbors who you know have a hammer. One neighbor never allows anyone to borrow anything or use any of his stuff without paying up. This neighbor represents a closed or proprietary system. Another neighbor leaves his garage open and allows you to take anything you need without any rules or guidelines. This is your bearded open-source neighbor. The third neighbor represents an API. You can utilize the services of her hammer as long as you ask her in the proper way. Furthermore, she doesn't actually give it to you; she just allows you to use it.

III. WHAT IS A WEB SERVICE API?

A web service API is an API designed for specific web applications. Web service APIs are one of the hallmarks of the current web ecosystem: an ecosystem based on openness and sharing. Post to Facebook, tweet this, Tumblr that, and so on. The web services we use are no longer closed, autonomous systems. They work together, data flowing freely between them. This is achieved through the use of web service APIs.

IV. TECHNICAL SETUP

Before you will be able to follow along with the examples in this book, you will need to be able to write and post files to the web. For that you will need the following:

1. A web server to which you have write access. Contact your system administrator to get set up with web server space.

2. PHP scripting language, which must be installed on your web server. There is a very good chance that it already is. Contact your system administrator to make sure.

3. A text editor. For beginners I would recommend TextWrangler for Mac or Notepad++ for Windows. For more advanced coders, I would recommend using VI or VIM in the Terminal (Mac) with shell access.

4. An FTP/SFTP client. Many text editors such as TextWrangler have a built-in FTP/SFTP client that allows you to edit your scripts and seamlessly save them to the web server.

The best way to get set up is to speak with your systems folks. They'll be able to get you started with your web development environment.

V. TECHNICAL PRIMER

If you have a solid basic understanding of HTML and PHP, then you can skip this section. Beginners, however, should read through this section. I will introduce the basic HTML and PHP concepts that will be employed throughout the examples in this book.

HTML

HTML is the language of the web. It is used to mark up the *content* of web pages. Most of the scripts written in this book are PHP driven, but we will be using some HTML elements. Therefore, we should introduce some basic concepts of HTML.

HTML Tags

HTML markup is built around the use of HTML tags. Let's start with the basics.

The DOCTYPE declaration is the first tag in an HTML document. It informs the browser which HTML version the web page will be employing:

```
<!DOCTYPE html PUBLIC "-//W3C//DTD XHTML 1.0 Transitional//EN" "http://www.w3
    .org/TR/xhtml1/DTD/xhtml1-transitional.dtd">
```

Next comes the `<html>` tag. All HTML files must include this tag at the top of the document, usually beneath the DOCTYPE declaration. The closing `</html>` tag will be the last tag in the document.

The head section of a web page is enclosed in `<head></head>` tags. This section usually contains the `<title>` of the web page, links to external files such as CSS or JavaScript files, and other metadata.

The body of the HTML document follows the head. Most of the elements within the `<body></body>` tags will be visible on the browser page.

Sections within the body of a web page are denoted by heading tags. The largest heading tag is `<h1>`, so any text between `<h1>` and `</h1>` will be larger than the rest of the text on the page. You can use smaller heading tags by changing the number after *h*: a slightly smaller heading tag would be `<h2>` and so forth—up to `<h6>`.

Paragraphs in an HTML document are enclosed within `<p></p>` tags. When we extract data via APIs later in the book, we will make that data visible within HTML paragraphs and will thus be using this tag quite a bit.

Basic lists are indicated with `<ul></ul>` tags. Much of the data that we will be working with will be in the form of lists—of book titles, tweets, and so forth—and we will be displaying that data in list form on our web pages. Each item in a list is further enclosed within `<li></li>` tags.

Line breaks are indicated by a single `<br />` tag. This tag can also be used to place empty lines within an HTML document for spacing purposes.

You've probably noticed by now that nearly all HTML elements include both opening and closing tags. Thus if you start a paragraph with an opening `<p>` tag, you must end it—after you've put in your text—with a closing `</p>` tag. Note, too, that HTML tags should be lowercase at all times: `<h1>`, not `<H1>`.

Sample HTML Document

After you have set up your web development environment with your systems administrator, you might want to create a basic HTML document and upload it to your web server space to ensure that everything is set up properly.

Open up your text editor and create a file called `hello_world` and save it as an HTML document before proceeding.

Type the following in to your text editor:

```
<!DOCTYPE html PUBLIC "-//W3C//DTD XHTML 1.0 Transitional//EN" "http://www.w3
    .org/TR/xhtml1/DTD/xhtml1-transitional.dtd">
<html>
<head>
<title>Hello World!!</title>
</head>
<body>
<h1>My First HTML Document</h1>
<p>Here is a paragraph of text.</p>
<br />
<p>Here is another paragraph of text that introduces a list of items.</p>
<ul>
<li>first list item</li>
<li>second list item</li>
<li>third list item</li>
</ul>
</body>
</html>
```

Now, open up a browser and go to this file on your web server. You should see an HTML page that looks like this:

My First HTML Document

Here is a paragraph of text.

Here is another paragraph of text that introduces a list of items.

- first list item
- second list item
- third list item

Now that we have the web environment set up and you understand the basics of HTML, let's move on to the core concepts of PHP that will be employed in this book.

PHP Concepts

PHP, or Hypertext Preprocessor, is a widely used general-purpose scripting language that can be embedded within HTML. All of the files that we create will be PHP files, so you must have PHP installed on your web server for these scripts to work properly.

PHP files begin with a simple PHP declaration:

```
<?php
```

and end with a closing tag:

```
?>
```

Print

The PHP `print` function will print to a web page whatever is contained within quotation marks.

Let's create our first PHP file. Open up your text editor and create a file called `hello_world` and save it as a PHP file. Enter the following text into your file:

```
<?php
print '<h1>Hello World!</h1>';
?>
```

Notice that the `print` line ends with a semicolon. Nearly all lines of code in a PHP script end with a semicolon. Exceptions include PHP logic such as `if` and `for` statements. We will get into this later.

Variables

Variables are used to store data in a convenient way to use and reuse throughout a PHP document. We will use PHP variables quite a bit in the examples in this book. Declaring a static variable is very simple. Variables always start with `$` and should contain only lowercase text.

Let's declare a simple variable. Open up the PHP file you just created and delete the following line:

```
print '<h1>Hello World!</h1>';
```

Replace it with this:

```
$variable = "This is a variable.";
```

The variable entitled `$variable` can now be used throughout the document. To see how this works let's do a couple of things to the variable. First let's just print it out. We will be printing out variables throughout this book:

```
print '<h1>' . $variable . '</h1>';
```

Save the PHP file and open it in your browser. You should see plain text that says: This is a variable.

You can achieve the same effect by using the echo command:

```
echo $variable;
```

We will employ `echo` a lot in this book to ensure we have our variables correct.

Commenting Out Code

While we work on our scripts, it will sometimes be necessary to disable certain lines of code. This is a common coding need. This is done by *commenting out* code. Let's say that while we are working on a script, we are using the `echo` command quite a bit. This is useful for debugging purposes, but for production we don't want some of those variables `echo`'d out to the browser.

To comment out code we can do one of two things. We can comment out a single line of code by preceding the line with two forward slashes:

```
//echo $variable;
```

PHP will see the two slashes and not perform any PHP commands on that line. If your code spans more than one line, you can use the forward slash and asterisk technique:

```
/* print '<pre>';
print_r ($variable);
print '</pre>';
*/
```

This will comment out all of the content between the opening /* and ending */. This can be done for any amount of code that's more than one line.

Arrays

Much of the data that we work with is data stored in PHP arrays. We will not be building arrays, but we will be working with them.

PHP arrays are ordered maps that associate values to keys. To get a basic idea of what an array is, let's make a simple array to work with:

```
$array = array(1,2,3,4,5);
print_r ($array);
```

The command used to print out arrays is print_r. Save the file and open it in your browser. The array should be seen as follows:

```
Array ( [0] => 1 [1] => 2 [2] => 3 [3] => 4 [4] => 5 )
```

The number within brackets is the key, while the number following the => is the value. We will be working with arrays quite a bit in this book.

Logic

PHP allows us to use logic on our variables to make decisions. The two primary logic functions that we will use are if and for.

if Logic

Let's create a new variable to use for an example of how if is employed:

```
$var = "1";
```

So $var equals one. Let's use if:

```
if $var == "1" {
echo $var;
}
```

After our `if` command is the variable that we are checking—in this case `$var`. We are checking to see if `$var` equals one, so we use the `==` operator, which means "is equal to." In quotes is the value that we are checking for. Next we have an opening curly bracket. Notice that we do not have a closing semicolon after the curly bracket. Anything contained in the curly brackets will be completed if the variable equals one. In this case we are just echoing out the variable. Every `if` command must end with a closing curly bracket.

We will be using only the `==` operator in the examples throughout the book. For a complete list of PHP comparison operators see the PHP Manual (at http://php.net/manual/en/language.operators.comparison.php).

`for` Logic

We can use `for` logic to loop through and print out the values of arrays, something we will be dealing with quite a bit in this book.

Let's take another look at the array we created earlier:

```
$array = array(1,2,3,4,5);
```

In order to use `for` logic, we need to know how many values are in the arrays that we are working with. To do that we can employ the `count` command:

```
$count = count($array)
```

What we are doing here is storing the number of values in the `$array` array in another array called `$count`. To ensure that this is working properly, echo out the `$count`:

```
echo $count;
```

Save your PHP file and open it in the browser. You should see a number. It should be 5, if you created the array as mentioned earlier.

Now we can use that variable in a `for` logic loop:

```
for ($i = 0; $i < $count; $i++) {
echo $array[$i];
}
```

When you save this and open it in the browser, you should see the values of the array printed out in order: 12345.

If you wanted to put a line break between the values, you could change what happens within the `for` loop:

```
for ($i = 0; $i < $count; $i++) {
```

```
echo $array[$i];
echo '<br />';
}
```

Let's break the `for` loop down. First we have the `for` command followed by a variable and some commands in parentheses. In the parentheses we are declaring a variable `$i` and assigning it an initial value of 0. Then, after a semicolon, we are saying that while `$i` is less than the value of the `$count` we obtained earlier (i.e., 5), then do what is in the curly brackets. Lastly, we are telling the `for` loop to add 1 to `$i` after each time through the loop. So after it goes through the loop once, `$i` will change its value from 0 to 1, then from 1 to 2, and so forth, until it is no longer less than 5. Once that happens the `for` loop will stop.

This allows PHP to work through the array and for each value in the array to perform the commands in the brackets. Thus for each value in the array it is printing it out and following it with a line break `<br />`.

Data Types

The information that is sent to us via the varied APIs in this book comes in the form of data structures. The two primary data types that we will be working with are JSON (JavaScript Object Notation) and XML. JSON is simpler to work with using PHP and requires only a few built-in PHP functions to parse into PHP arrays. XML data requires some extra massaging of the data to get to a point where we can use it.

HTTP Request

All of the APIs that we are working with are based on HTTP requests. You are familiar with HTTP because you use it every time you visit a web page. The data that we are requesting from the various web services is sent to us via HTTP. You will see that one of the first things we do in each script that we write is to create a URL variable for that web service.

The Elements of a Typical Web Service API

The two primary elements that are inherent to all web service APIs are data and methods. There is considerable variation among the different APIs as to the specifics of these elements, but all APIs will involve data and methods. In addition, some APIs require API keys or authentication, or both. We will take a look at those elements in the individual API chapters. Let's first take a look at the data and the formats you will encounter.

API Data

The format of the data that is provided through most APIs is typically XML (REST, SOAP), JSON, RSS, Atom, and serialized PHP. Web service APIs that provide more than one format option facilitate greater developer flexibility. Here is an example of XML data returned through the Twitter API:

```xml
<statuses type="array">
 <status>
    <created_at>Wed May 04 23:39:19 +0000 2011</created_at>
    <id>65923490921984000</id>
    <text>Let's get Jen to 200 tweets! Yahoo! http://t.co/qUBlS2d</text>
    <source>
       <a href="http://twitter.com/tweetbutton" rel="nofollow">Tweet Button</a>
    </source>
    <truncated>false</truncated>
    <favorited>false</favorited>
    <in_reply_to_status_id/>
    <in_reply_to_user_id/>
    <in_reply_to_screen_name/>
    <retweet_count>0</retweet_count>
    <retweeted>false</retweeted>
    <user>
       <id>292398272</id>
       <name>Brad Klassen</name>
       <screen_name>logo_man</screen_name>
       <location/>
       <description/>
       <profile_image_url>
        http://a1.twimg.com/profile_images/1337753208/009_normal.JPG
       </profile_image_url>
       <url/>
       <protected>false</protected>
       <followers_count>1</followers_count>
       <profile_background_color>C0DEED</profile_background_color>
       <profile_text_color>333333</profile_text_color>
       <profile_link_color>0084B4</profile_link_color>
       <profile_sidebar_fill_color>DDEEF6</profile_sidebar_fill_color>
       <profile_sidebar_border_color>C0DEED</profile_sidebar_border_color>
       <friends_count>3</friends_count>
       <created_at>Tue May 03 15:51:05 +0000 2011</created_at>
    </user>
 </status>
</statuses>
```

SANDBOX EXAMPLE 1

Let's access Twitter's public status time line. Enter the API request URL into your browser:

```
http://api.twitter.com/1/statuses/public_timeline.format
```

Now replace `format` with `xml`. You should see data similar to the XML data in the example above. Now try entering `rss` or `atom`. The data you see now should look a bit more familiar to you, especially if you are used to subscribing to RSS feeds. Most APIs are flexible enough to give you multiple format options so that, depending on your project, you can choose the one that works best.

API Methods

How do developers manipulate data via an API? Primarily through simple HTTP GET and POST requests. For example, the data above was retrieved via an HTTP GET request using the following URL template:

```
http://api.twitter.com/1/statuses/public_timeline.format
```

Each API has several methods to access different types of data. For example, the above method retrieved the public time line of statuses of all Twitter users. Other methods allow you to retrieve other data such as Twitter trends.[2] The individual chapters in this book will explicate these methods in detail.

VI. WHY ARE APIs IMPORTANT FOR LIBRARIES?

APIs are important for libraries because they allow them to connect with the wider web ecosystem and to integrate with prominent web services such as Twitter, Flickr, Facebook, and more. The current social media environment is one of interconnectedness. APIs allow libraries to join in that interconnectedness.

In addition to this overarching benefit, APIs have the ability to change library workflows and enhance existing services. For example, working with the Twitter API, libraries can automatically tweet to a specific Twitter user when a study room becomes available, or set up a web-based dashboard that allows users and staff to see if there are any computer or printer problems (see chapter 1).

VII. CHAPTER STRUCTURE

For ease of use, each chapter is structured in the same manner. Each begins with a discussion of services that could be provided through the use of the respective API. This section is followed by a thorough explanation of the API. Finally, each chapter features an "API in Action" section that details the construction of an application in a step-by-step manner. (One exception: chapter 3 is organized around a real-life case study involving the Vimeo API.)

For those of you who like lists, here's another look at what each chapter offers:

- Potential services achieved through use of the API
- Real-life examples of how the API is being used in libraries
- Technical explanation of the API
- API in Action: a step-by-step construction of the application

Note that most of the applications we create together will lack the styling and presentation that comes with further web development using CSS and HTML. Instead of focusing on aesthetic presentation with our scripts, we will be learning how to gather, parse, and deliver data.

VIII. ADDITIONAL RESOURCES

I will be guiding you step-by-step through each script, so you can reasonably work through them without consulting other resources. However, you may want to refer to other resources to clarify certain functions or to answer any questions you may have. I list here some of the better places to go for such information.

HTML

HTML Tutorial, www.w3schools.com/html/.

W3Schools.com is a very good resource to help one learn the basics of many web technologies, not just HTML. Each technology is presented through a series of step-by-step tutorials with a "Try it Yourself" editor that allows you to write code and see the results in your browser without the need to set up a web server. In addition to these two features, W3Schools.com also has an extensive reference section and glossary.

PHP

- PHP Tutorial, www.w3schools.com/php/.
- PHP Manual, www.php.net/manual/en/.

The PHP Manual offers complete explanations of all of the functions and operators we use for the scripts that we construct throughout this book. This is the official site for PHP.

- Welling, Luke, and Laura Thomson. *PHP and MySQL Web Development*. 4th ed. Upper Saddle River, NJ: Addison-Wesley, 2008.
  A very good introduction to the concept of database-driven dynamic coding with PHP, this book complements many of the concepts and scripts we explore throughout this book.

Twitter API

- https://dev.twitter.com/.
  This is the official website for the Twitter development community. Any bugs or changes to the API will be reported upon and discussed here. Each API function is delineated in full detail. This resource should be continually open in your browser as you work through the Twitter API section.

- Makice, Kevin. *Twitter API: Up and Running*. Sebastopol, CA: O'Reilly Media, 2009. http://shop.oreilly.com/product/9780596154622.do.
  Another great introductory work specifically for the Twitter API. Though Makice's examples are not specific to libraries, his work explains in great detail the core concepts we cover in this book.

Flickr API

- www.flickr.com/services/api/.
  This is the official website for Flickr's API. Along with technical documents on all aspects of the API, there is a great Flickr developer community that can be tapped into through this resource.

- Richardson, Leonard, and Sam Ruby. *RESTful Web Services*. Sebastopol, CA: O'Reilly, 2007. http://shop.oreilly.com/product/9780596529260.do.

Vimeo API

https://developer.vimeo.com/.
  The official web resource for Vimeo's API and development platform. The code that we write throughout the Vimeo chapter is well documented on this site.

Google Charts API

https://developers.google.com/chart/.

OCLC Web Services

http://oclc.org/developer/webservices.

HathiTrust API

www.hathitrust.org/data_api.

Open Library API
http://openlibrary.org/developers/api.

LibraryThing API
www.librarything.com/api.

Goodreads API
www.goodreads.com/api.

Google Books API
https://developers.google.com/books/docs/v1/using.

NOTES

1. David Orenstein, "QuickStudy: Application Programming Interface (API)," *Computerworld*, January 10, 2000, www.computerworld.com/s/article/43487 /Application_Programming_Interface.

2. "GET trends/:woeid," https://dev.twitter.com/docs/api/1/get/trends/%3Awoeid.

CHAPTER ONE

TWITTER API AND LIBRARIES

Twitter's API offers much functionality that libraries can exploit.

Reminders and Alerts

We know that younger Americans rely less and less on e-mail, so imagine your catalog tweeting to a patron that a certain book has been returned and is available! Or imagine a study room reservation system that tweets out availability and reminders to patrons.

Equipment Status Updates

Twitter almost seems custom built for status updates about printers and other library equipment. The Miami University Libraries, for example, rely on a printer outage alert system that uses the Twitter API. When a printer is down, a librarian will tweet about it using specific hashtags (e.g., #king is #down). This tweet triggers a script that updates a web-based dashboard displaying the status of printers. Other staff members should now be aware of the problem and can take the necessary steps to ensure that patrons get the copies they need during the downtime. The same tweet will also alert printer vendors to come and fix the problem. Once the problem's been fixed, another tweet goes out (e.g., #king is #up). This tweet, like the first one, updates the printer status dashboard, alerting everyone that the printer is again available.

Computer Availability

As libraries become technology hubs for academic institutions and municipalities, managing computer resources is becoming a priority. Because the supply of resources is often less than demand, an alert system could be a huge benefit, especially to users who rely on libraries for their computing needs.

Some academic libraries have developed web-based interfaces that display real-time computer availability for their users.[1] This concept could be integrated with Twitter's API to create notifications for individual Twitter users. For example, @jpmichel could tell the computer availability application that he would like to be notified when any Mac computer is available or even when a *specific* Mac computer is available.

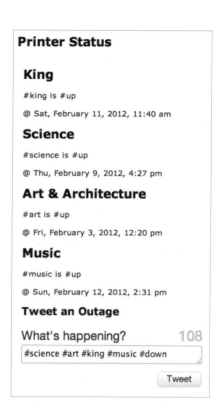

Curated Social Media

A core task for librarians has been to manage the information resources that our users demand and to provide access to that information. In this current information paradigm, where the web rules, that task is extremely difficult if not impossible. But again, APIs give developers the ability to create applications that present web resources on a particular topic in an easily understandable interface. For lack of a better term, we can think of these applications as *curated web resources*.

As an example, let's say that a class is studying U.S.–Arab relations. Typically, librarians will guide students to databases, books, and possibly multimedia materials. But will they guide them to good, reliable, insightful web resources? Will they guide them to authoritative Twitter users?

APIs could be used to create applications that list Tweets, YouTube and Vimeo videos, Flickr images, and other items that are pertinent to U.S.–Arab relations, further enriching the user's experience.

This concept could be extended to local issues as well. Is there a crucial vote coming up on education? Libraries could provide a one-stop place for materials relating to the issue: books, journal and newspaper articles, tweets, videos, images, and more.

Local User Data Mining for Inroads into Proactive Service

Many libraries now use Twitter to engage with their user base. The success of this endeavor depends on the level of interaction between the library and the users. Ideally, Twitter interactions should be genuine and on a daily basis. Tweeting out a new book feed or event announcements is not enough and doesn't take advantage of the true nature of Twitter. To engage in a genuine way on a consistent basis can be difficult and time-consuming since staff would need to first follow as many users as possible but then also monitor the Twitter feed, looking for opportunities to engage. By utilizing the API, you can produce an application that scours your geographic region for Twitter users who are tweeting about things that relate to the library in some sense. Essentially, the API would data-mine the tweets within a specified geographical radius for a list of keywords that in some way relate to the library—*book, research, study, homework, newspapers, library,* and so on—and present the tweets in a unified interface. This application would give staff nothing but relevant tweets from which engaging discussions can spring.

TWITTER API TECHNICAL DETAILS

Twitter API Overview

As of this publication, the Twitter API actually consists of three separate APIs, a problem Twitter plans to fix in the future. The three APIs are the Twitter REST API, the Search API, and the Streaming API. I will cover each API below.

As mentioned in the introduction, the Twitter APIs are based on simple HTTP GET and POST requests. Supported data formats for the Twitter APIs are JSON, XML, RSS, and Atom. Most of the applications that developers in the library world will focus on will be basic status updating and viewing applications. The Twitter APIs have dozens of methods, but for the purposes of this book, I will focus on what's most important for the library world.

Twitter REST API

The Twitter REST API gives programmers access to core Twitter data such as update time lines, status updates, and user information.

Twitter Search API

As opposed to the Twitter REST API, the Search API has only one method: `search`. The Search API is based on a simple GET request using the following URL template and returns either JSON or Atom:

```
http://search.twitter.com/search.format
```

The Search API also accepts a variety of parameters or arguments. These parameters are concatenated to the end of the URL using the following format:

```
http://search.twitter.com/search.format?q=search-term&parameter=parameter-value
```

Available parameters for the Search API are as follows:

PARAMETER	MEANING	REQUIRED
q	Search query	Yes
callback	Defines a callback function	No; must use JSON format
lang	Language, using a two-letter code defined by ISO 639-1	No
rpp	Number of tweets per page	No
page	Page number to return	No
since_id	Returns tweets with IDs greater than specified ID	No
until	Returns tweets before a given date, in YYYY-MM-DD format	No
geocode	Returns tweets within a give radius (mi or km) of a certain latitude and longitude	No
show_user	Prepends "user:" to beginning of tweet	No
result_type	Mixed, recent, or popular	No

Twitter Streaming API

The Twitter Streaming API is for developers interested in building applications that allow users to see an ongoing stream of tweets. An example of this API's usage is Esri GIS software for displaying real-time earthquake data.[2]

TWITTER API IN ACTION

Printer/Equipment Status Application

Let's start building! This step-by-step instruction will build a Twitter application that allows staff members to both view the statuses of printers (up or down) and alert technical staff that printers are having a problem, prompting them to come and fix the issue.

For this application we will utilize the Twitter REST API and write the script using PHP. Whereas before, you entered the HTTP requests as URLs in your browser, we will now use those URL requests in a PHP script.

In order to properly implement this example, you must have some Twitter data. So either create a Twitter account and post some tweets or use the data from this example. At the Miami University Libraries, we set up a Twitter account expressly for the purpose of relating printer statuses to librarians, technical staff, and circulation staff. Let's take a closer look at how this system works.

First, when a printing problem is detected the librarian working at the information desk will tweet from the printing Twitter account (@mulp4p) that a printer at a specific location is down. We have set up the use of hashtags to provide uniformity that will come into play during the API development. As an example, if a printer is down in our main location, King Library, the librarian might tweet: #king is #down continual jamming. The location of the problem and whether it is up or down are always preceded by a hashtag. After that initial statement, the librarian can provide a short synopsis of the problem.

Next, our printing technical staff is notified of the printing problem because they've been set up to receive tweets on their mobile devices. Once they've fixed the problem, they will tweet: #king is #up.

What we are doing with the Twitter API is essentially creating a dashboard display that lets users see the statuses of all of our printing locations at a glance. If the printer is up (usual case), there will be a smiley face GIF next to the tweet saying that the printer is up followed by the date and time of that tweet. If a printer is

---

SANDBOX EXAMPLE 2

Let's see what the popular tweets are in your neighborhood. We can do this using the Twitter Search API. First go to http://itouchmap.com/latlong.html to grab your latitude and longitude. Once you've got these, enter the following URL into your browser, replacing `latitude,longitude` with the actual numbers:

```
http://search.twitter.com/search.atom?q=*&geocode=latitude,longitude,5mi
```

The `*` returns all tweets, but try replacing it with a search term or multiple search terms separated by the `+` sign.

Play around with this URL request format by utilizing different parameters and values. Pretty cool, huh?

down, there will be an icon of a printer with a warning sign next to it and the text of the tweet followed by the date and time.

The data that we want to utilize and display are the tweets coming from a particular Twitter account that we've created for a printing team expressly for this purpose. The first step is to get the data. This is where the simple HTTP requests come into play. We will use the `statuses/user_timeline` method. So the initial piece of code in your PHP script will be

```php
<?php
$info_url = "http://api.twitter.com/1/statuses/user_timeline.json?user
    _id=191130352&count=200";
```

Let's break this line down. First, we have the variable `$info_url`. This variable will contain the HTTP request. Next, we have the API request method:

```
http://api.twitter.com/1/statuses/user_timeline.json
```

This request method returns the time line of status updates by a particular Twitter user. The format of the data is specified after `user_timeline`. In this case the format of the data we will be utilizing is JSON. The other data format choices you have for this request method are XML, Atom, and RSS.

Finally, we have a couple of parameters. In this case the parameters are `user_id` and `count`. The parameter `user_id` gets us the data from the Twitter account that we have set up for our printing team. To pull data that you are interested in just substitute `191130352` with the `user_id` you need. An easy way to find the `user_id` for your account is to go to www.idfromuser.com/. The parameter `count` tells the Twitter API how many tweets you want to retrieve. You can enter any number up to 200. Now we're ready for our next line of code:

```php
$raw_data = file_get_contents($info_url);
```

This line actually gets all of the data from the HTTP request method, stored in `$info_url`, and stores it in the variable `$raw_data`. At this point, I'd like you to view the data that is being pulled via the code we've scripted so far. So in the next line enter the following piece of code:

```php
print '<pre>';
print_r ($raw_data);
print '</pre>';
?>
```

Upload this PHP file to a web server and view it in a browser. You should now see the raw JSON data of the respective users' tweets.

Erase or comment out that bit of code and let's get back to business. The next line of code is

```
$data = json_decode($raw_data);
```

This piece of code will take the messy JSON data that you just saw and reformat it into an array so that it's easier to parse further on in this script. After you enter this line, reinsert or uncomment the code from above and change `$raw_data` to `$data`:

```
print '<pre>';
print_r ($data);
print '</pre>';
?>
```

Take a look at the script again in the browser. See how much more clarity there is in the data structure? So now that we have the data available to us in a nice array, how do we pull out pieces that we want, as opposed to just displaying all of the data?

To begin, first comment out these three lines of code:

```
print '<pre>';
print_r ($data);
print '</pre>';
```

Now, after `$data = json_decode($raw_data);` type the following code:

```
print '<p>' . $data[0]->text . '</p>';
```

What you should see is the text of one tweet only. Now try adding other fields that were displayed in the full array. For example, try outputting `screen_name` and `created_at`:

```
print '<p>' . $data[0]->screen_name . '</p>';
print '<p>' . $data[0]->created_at . '</p>';
```

What happens when you execute the above code in a browser? There's no screen name, is there? That's because each of the tweets presented to us via the API is in a PHP object, meaning there are multiple arrays within one major array. To get at the `screen_name` field, you must get into the `user` array. So delete this line:

```
print '<p>' . $data[0]->screen_name . '</p>';
```

and replace it with this one:

```
print '<p>' . $data[0]->user->screen_name . '</p>';
```

Now, when executed, you should see the text of the tweet, the screen name, and finally the creation date.

This is cool and all, but how useful is one tweet? Ultimately, you will most likely be interested in displaying or parsing through multiple tweets. So instead of outputting the text of one tweet, let's output all of our tweets. To do this you will need to implement a PHP `for` loop. This means that while conditions are true, or more specifically, while there are tweets to be outputted, your code will output data. This will be a very simple example. To execute a `for` loop, we must first know how many PHP objects exist (including individual tweets and the metadata). To do this type the following code:

```
$count = count($data);
```

Now, that we've got the number of objects stored in a variable let's add the first line of the PHP `for` loop:

```
for ($i = 0; $i < $count; $i++)
```

So, what is this doing? There are three pieces of logic occurring within the parentheses: First, we are establishing that our variable `$i = 0`. Second, we are telling the script to execute the code that will follow as long as `$i` is less than the `$count` variable. Remember that when this loop begins, `$i` is 0 and `$count` is somewhere between 200 and 1. Finally, we are telling the script to add 1 to `$i` each time it goes through the loop. So when the code goes through the loop once, `$i` becomes 1. When it goes through it again it becomes 2, and so forth, until the loop finally ends, when `$i` is no longer less than `$count`.

Now that we've established the parameters for the loop, what is the script supposed to do while `$i` is less than `$count`? Those instructions are always stored within curly brackets:

```
for ($i = 0; $i < $count; $i++) {
print '<p>' . $data[$i]->text . '</p>';
}
```

Execute this above code and view it in the browser. You should see nothing but the text of all of your tweets.

Can you see how this is iteratively working through the object? Recall the code you used to output all of the Twitter data:

```
print '<pre>';
print_r ($data);
print '</pre>';
```

Each PHP object (represented here by the generic `stdClass` PHP object) started with

```
[0] => stdClass Object
```

with the number in brackets increasing incrementally down the line, so the next PHP object was

```
[1] => stdClass Object
```

and so forth.

Let's look again at the `for` loop:

```
for ($i = 0; $i < $count; $i++) {
print '<p>' . $data[$i]->text . '</p>';
}
```

So when the `for` loop begins, the code is printing `$data[0]`, which is the first object; the next time the loop happens `$i` is increased from 0 to 1, which makes the code print `$data[1]`, and so forth.

Now that you know how to display your tweets, you can start thinking about what tweets you want to display using simple PHP logic. In the example we've been working on, we want to display only those tweets that relate whether a certain printing location is having a problem and if it has been fixed.

So let's see how, using the API and simple PHP logic, we can pull out only certain tweets, wrap them in HTML, and apply CSS style to them. We'll start again with the `for` loop:

```
for ($i = 0; $i < $count; $i++) {
```

Within this `for` loop we're going to create some new variables to keep things simple; apply regular expressions to determine if the tweets contain the hashtags we are looking for; put tweets for the different locations into separate arrays; then apply CSS divs and output the display in HTML. The next few lines are

```
$string = $data[$i]->text;
$time = strtotime($data[$i]->created_at);
$tweet_time = date("D, F j, Y, g:i a", $time);
```

The first line is creating a variable `$string` for the text of the tweets (again, `text` is the field for the actual words in the tweet). It's just much simpler to use `$string` as opposed to `$data[$i]->text`.

The next two lines are working with the `created_at` field to produce a date and time display that makes more sense to users. The first of these lines of code is taking the string contained in `$data[$i]->created_at` and converting it to a UNIX timestamp, then the second line takes that timestamp and reformats it into a more readable date and time. These lines of code converted this:

Mon May 16 19:45:19 +0000 2011

to this:

Mon, May 16, 2011, 3:45 pm

a much easier string to read.

The next bit of code determines if the text of the tweet contains the hashtag #king and either #up or #down. If the tweet does not contain one of these hashtags, it will disregard the tweet and not display it. This is important because the Twitter account can be used for other types of tweets as well, and we only want to display those tweets that pertain to the status of the printers. The code begins with some `if` logic:

```
if ((preg_match('/#\bking\b/', $string)) && ((preg_match('/#\bup\b/', $string))
    | (preg_match('/#\bdown\b/', $string)))) {
```

This line of code is saying that if within the variable `$string` (which, again, is the text of the individual tweets) there is the hashtag #king *and* (`&&`) either (`|`) the hashtag #up or #down, then perform the code that follows within curly brackets `{ }`. That code is

```
$tweets_king = $string;
$king_array[] = $tweets_king;
```

Now that I've determined that only those tweets that contain #king will be used, we can place those tweets into a King-specific variable called `$tweets_king`. Next, we can take that variable and iteratively build a King-specific array of tweet texts. That is achieved in the second line of code.

Now we want to do the same thing as in the previous two lines, except we need to manipulate the time of the tweets as opposed to the text:

```
$time_king = $tweet_time;
$king_time_array[] = $time_king;
}
```

So now we have a simple array of the text of King-specific tweets, `$king_array[]`, and a simple array of King-specific timestamps, `$king_time_array[]`.

Now that we have the data we need to display in nice arrays, we can begin displaying that data. As mentioned earlier, I am supplying a different icon depending on whether the printers are up or down. To do this I've created two separate CSS divs with different styles. These next few lines of code will determine which CSS div to apply and print out:

```php
if (preg_match('/#\bup\b/', $king_array[0])) {
print '<div class="printer_status_up"><h2>King</h2>';
}
if (preg_match('/#\bdown\b/', $king_array[0])) {
print '<div class="printer_status_down"><h2>King</h2>';
}
```

First, the code is looking into the array of king tweets `$king_array[0]` and checking to see if it contains the hashtag up or down. Remember that the tweets will contain one or the other at this point as determined a few lines earlier in the code. If it contains the hashtag #up it is printing out the CSS div class `printer_status_up` followed by an `<h2>` with the word "King."

If the tweet contains the hashtag #down, it replaces the div class with `printer_status_down`.

At this point we have the correct icon printed out (background image of the CSS div) and a heading saying "King." Now we just need to print out the text of the tweet and the time it was posted:

```php
print '<div class="p_status_details">
    <p>'. $king_array[0] .'</p>
    <p>@ '. $king_time_array[0] .'</p></div>'
print '</div>';
```

There we are. To recap: using the Twitter API REST method of `user_time line`, we were able to harvest the metadata attached to all of the tweets coming from an individual user. Then, using PHP logic, we determined which tweets were relevant to our application and displayed them using HTML and CSS.

Here's the entire script:

```php
<?php
$info_url = "http://api.twitter.com/1/statuses/user_timeline.json?user_id=191130352";
$raw_data = file_get_contents($info_url);
$data = json_decode($raw_data);
$count = count($data);
for ($i = 0; $i < $count; $i++){
```

```
    $string = $data[$i]->text;
    $time = strtotime($data[$i]->created_at);
    $tweet_time = date("D, F j, Y, g:i a", $time);
    if ((preg_match('/#\bking\b/', $string)) && ((preg_match('/#\bup\b/',
        $string)) | (preg_match('/#\bdown\b/', $string)))) {
        $tweets_king = $string;
        $king_array[] = $tweets_king;
        $time_king = $tweet_time;
        $king_time_array[] = $time_king;
        }
    }
if (preg_match('/#\bup\b/', $king_array[0])) {
    print '<div class="printer_status_up"><h2>King</h2>';
    }
if (preg_match('/#\bdown\b/', $king_array[0])) {
    print '<div class="printer_status_down"><h2>King</h2>';
    }
print '<div class="p_status_details">
    <p>'. $king_array[0] .'</p>
    <p>@ '. $king_time_array[0] .'</p></div>';
print '</div>';
?>
```

Local User Data Mining Application

This API in Action section will produce a web application that displays local user tweets that mention keywords such as books, library, research, and studying. This app is designed to act as a springboard to meaningful, engaged contact with library users. Like the printer status application, this script takes advantage of Twitter's Search API.

To begin, let's create a new PHP file. The first lines will be

```
<?php
echo '<!DOCTYPE HTML PUBLIC "-//W3C//DTD HTML 4.01 Transitional//EN" "http://
    www.w3.org/TR/html4/loose.dtd">';
echo '<html>';
echo '<head>';
echo '<link rel="stylesheet" href="styles.css" type="text/css">';
echo '</head>';
```

Obviously, you can edit this `<head>` section as you see fit. The first important aspect of this script is to build an array of keywords that will bring back the most relevant and pertinent Tweets. We will be using generic terms, but you can tailor the application to meet your own needs by adding library branch names or other localized keywords.

```
$keywords = array (book,research,homework,study,writing,reading,library,
      libraries,experiment,'journal article');
$keywords_count = count($keywords);
```

Here we are counting the number of keywords in the `$keywords` array. This step is needed for the `for` loop, as follows:

```
for ($i = 0; $i < $keywords_count; $i++) {
```

Essentially this line indicates that for every keyword in the `$keywords` array do the following:

```
$info_url = "http://search.twitter.com/search.json?q=" .
      urlencode($keywords[$i]) . "&geocode=39.5069974,-84.745231,1mi";
```

Here our data is being pulled in from Twitter via HTTP GET. Notice that the first part of the URL matches the printer status application above (`http://search.twitter.com/search.json?q=`), but instead of hard-coding the search query we are iteratively adding keywords from the keyword array: `urlencode($keywords[$i])`. It is important to integrate the `urlencode` function into your PHP scripts. It cleans up strings intended for placement in URLs by fixing any white space and special character problems that may arise. Do it and rest easy.

Now let's clean up the JSON data brought back from the HTTP GET command above:

```
$raw_data = file_get_contents($info_url);
$data = json_decode($raw_data);
```

The `$data` variable now contains tweet data from one of the keyword queries. Let's take a look at the data that we've got so far:

```
print '<pre>';
print_r ($data);
print '</pre>';
}
```

Make sure you close out the `for` loop. If you now save your PHP file and open it in a browser, you should see PHP objects for each tweet returned on each keyword—something like this:

```
stdClass Object
(
[completed_in] => 0.529
[max_id] => 1.28114081172E+17
[max_id_str] => 128114081172430848
[next_page] => ?page=2&max_id=128114081172430848&q=book&geocode=39.5069974%2C
        -84.745231%2C5mi
[page] => 1
[query] => book
[refresh_url] => ?since_id=128114081172430848&q=book&geocode=39.5069974%2C
        -84.745231%2C5mi
[results] => Array
    (
        [0] => stdClass Object
        (
            [created_at] => Sun, 23 Oct 2011 14:22:31 +0000
            [from_user] => TomCedoz
            [from_user_id] => 248462697
            [from_user_id_str] => 248462697
            [geo] =>
            [location] => Oxford, Ohio
            [id] => 1.28114081172E+17
            [id_str] => 128114081172430848
            [iso_language_code] => en
            [metadata] => stdClass Object
                (
                    [result_type] => recent
                )
            [profile_image_url] => http://a1.twimg.com/profile_images/1594450363/3164
    40_10150867683150273_883190272_21167243_854313155_n_1__normal.jpg
            [source] => <a href="http://twitter.com/">web</a>
            [text] => @piersmorgan Book his flight to the states #MLSBound
            [to_user] => piersmorgan
            [to_user_id] => 4529414
            [to_user_id_str] => 4529414
        )
```

Here is all of the tweet data you have at your disposal to build your application.
Now let's go back to the script.

Delete or comment out this section before continuing:

```
/* print '<pre>';
print_r ($data);
print '</pre>';
}*/
```

For each keyword search, Twitter is returning an array of tweets that we need to count and then build another `for` loop to iteratively work through and ultimately display:

```
$count = count($data->results);
print '<h2>' . $keywords[$i] . '</h2>';
```

For each keyword that we have, we are printing out a header. This makes it easier to read on the interface.

```
for ($j = 0; $j < $count; $j++)
```

Here is the next `for` loop. Earlier we used a `for` loop to work through an array of keywords we built; this `for` loop works through the tweets returned on each keyword. So for every tweet, the script does the following:

```
{
    print '<p><a href="http://twitter.com/#!/' . urlencode($data->results[$j]
    ->from_user) . '">' . urlencode($data->results[$j]->from_user) . '</
    a>: ' . $data->results[$j]->text . '</p>';
}
}
?>
```

The script is printing out a list of tweets with the user name linked and the text of the tweet displayed. If executed properly, it should show you something like this but likely with more tweets:

book

scd: I have now preordered @austinkleon's new book.

GoCall_REAL: @iitzChelle_luv its a surprise lol! Nd no I got da same number! Nd yeah I got tht book! Nd NO yu can't use it! (;

CateCharvat: The only benefit of a prologue is being able to start a book & feel a sense of accomplishment with 20 pages down from the beginning #college

LaurennWeeeee: @Brittni_Graham dear I could get it up with a math book. Okayyy

nickcondeni: RT @BElting14: @Dr_AJPark @nickcondeni Scholastic Book Fair main feature

BElting14: @Dr_AJPark @nickcondeni Scholastic Book Fair main feature

PSEFoundation: Received my @Arjowiggins #52Weeks book today! Looking forward to being greener in new ways.

shanarosenberg: @laurenme0w absolutely LOVE LOVE my ereader. I'm sad when I have to read an actual paper book for some reason.

LauraLynnSmith: Read about her latest book in my interview w/the darling Betsy St. Amant on my Friday blog http://t.co/10ozdRTK

bookstumbrains: On The Blog: Review of Before I Fall by Lauren Oliver -- http://t.co/IvvAziKH

Swag_SurfinSeel: Finished hunger games book one.... Next one... Awaiting lending from mom. I'll never finish @dadseeley make it happen #technologyvrsmom

salonsignature: Book ahead CDB event and spring break is right around the corner.

BrickStOxford: RT @salonsignature: Salon Signature next week valentine day special book a haircut and receive a special gift..

gretchenpearson: Today's National Read in the Bathtub Day... Too bad I don't have a tub or a book...

salonsignature: Salon Signature next week valentine day special book a haircut and receive a special gift..

research

miamiulibraries: New Books: Conviction of the innocent : lessons from psychological research http://t.co/ATqmRCG

As you can see, we now can tap into our user base to find out what they are really thinking about studying and researching and the like, and we can potentially respond to tweets in a proactive way. A new reference service model is born.

Here is the complete, unadulterated script:

```php
<?php
echo '<!DOCTYPE HTML PUBLIC "-//W3C//DTD HTML 4.01 Transitional//EN" "http://
    www.w3.org/TR/html4/loose.dtd">';
echo '<html>';
echo '<head>';
echo '<link rel="stylesheet" href="styles.css" type="text/css">';
echo '</head>';
echo '<body>';
$keywords = array (book,research,homework,study,writing,reading,library,
    libraries,experiment,'journal article');
$keywords_count = count($keywords);
echo $keywords_count;
for ($i = 0; $i < $keywords_count; $i++) {
$info_url = "http://search.twitter.com/search.json?q=" .
    urlencode($keywords[$i]) . "&geocode=39.5069974,-84.745231,1mi";
$raw_data = file_get_contents($info_url);
$data = json_decode($raw_data);
$count = count($data->results);
print '<h2>' . $keywords[$i] . '</h2>';
for ($j = 0; $j < $count; $j++) {
    print '<p><a href="http://twitter.com/#!/' . urlencode($data->results[$j]->
        from_user) . '">' . urlencode($data->results[$j]->from_user) . '
        </a>: ' . $data->results[$j]->text . '</p>';
    }
}
echo '</body>';
echo '</html>';
?>
```

NOTES

1. For an example, see the interface for North Carolina State University's libraries at www.lib.ncsu.edu/compavailability/web.php.

2. See "Esri Enriches Maps with Tweets and the Streaming API," a case study involving the earthquake near Honshu, Japan, March 11, 2011, https://dev.twitter.com/case-studies /esri-enriches-maps-tweets-and-streaming-api.

CHAPTER TWO

FLICKR API AND LIBRARIES

There are many potential uses of Flickr's API for libraries.

Uploading Digital Collections to Flickr

In the past three years there has been much experimentation by academic libraries and special collections with respect to Flickr. That's not surprising, as Flickr is the go-to place on the web for photos and images. Again, imagining the web as a vast cityscape, Flickr is one of the large monoliths at the city's center.[1] These libraries, most notably, the Library of Congress, Oregon State University Libraries, the New York Public Library, and the Miami University Libraries, understand that, to date, the best way to expose digital image content to the widest audience is to upload to Flickr. By doing so, you not only benefit from Flickr's huge popularity but also from the visibility of its content to search engines.

Here's how the Library of Congress summed up its decision to upload to Flickr:

> Like any cultural heritage institution, the Library of Congress is always seeking to broaden the awareness of the resources that it collects, preserves, and makes accessible to the public to inspire, educate, and illuminate. The Library, a pioneer in the digitization of its collections, recognizes the power of the Web to enhance access and expose these resources to the world.

The library added that the project was pursued to solve problems inherent to all libraries in the digital age, namely:

a limit to institutional resources to provide detailed descriptions, historical context, and transcriptions of the thousands of items in large collections; a need to make the materials in those collections easily retrievable and accessible; competition for the attention of an online community that has ever expanding choices of where to pursue their interests, and a technical infrastructure that does not easily allow users to comment, share, and interact with content in the manner offered by popular social networking sites.[2]

Since the Library of Congress launched its Flickr project in 2008, many libraries have followed suit, uploading their massive digital collections. Fortunately, Flickr's API provides the necessary tools to accomplish this task.

Displaying Flickr Images on Local Library Websites

Utilizing the Flickr API, libraries can develop curated social media pages on their websites. We encountered this earlier in relation to Twitter, where we discussed the idea of filtering tweets related to a certain topic onto the library's website. Flickr images could be filtered onto the same web page. So, for example, let's say it's November 2012 and you have a page dedicated to the U.S. presidential election. On this page are library resources (i.e., books, videos, and journals), but users can also read tweets and view a slide show of Flickr images from the campaign trail.

FLICKR API TECHNICAL DETAILS

Flickr API Overview

Flickr's API, like Twitter's, is built upon simple HTTP GET and POST requests. Flickr also gives developers several options for request and response formats. The request formats are REST, XML-RPC, and SOAP; the response formats are REST, XML-RPC, SOAP, JSON, and PHP.

Flickr offers over 100 different API methods, allowing developers to get data ranging from simple image data to geolocation data. The two types of applications most relevant to libraries are those that use methods for uploading large image sets and those used for searching for and displaying images. I will discuss the Upload API in the Flickr API in Action section, but first let's take a look at the API method for searching for and displaying images.

When developing a search and display application for libraries, the REST request method is the most straightforward and approachable. The one significant difference between the Twitter and Flickr APIs is that for even the most basic of API applications, developers need to obtain an API key. The process is relatively simple. You will need to give your application a name and short description and also indicate whether you are creating a web-based application or a desktop application.

SANDBOX EXAMPLE 3

In this example, we will use the REST method flickr.photos.search to search for, sort, and display Flickr images based on a keyword or text string of our choosing. To begin, create a new PHP file:

```php
<?php
$info_url = "http://api.flickr.com/services/rest/?method=flickr.photos
    .search";
```

As you can see, in this example we are starting the script in the same fashion as the Twitter API in Action script—by setting a variable to the URL for the proper API method. Also as we did for the Twitter API, we will now append arguments[3] to the base URL:

```php
$api_key = "71632157deb60cd1fe5————————";
$text = "rose";
$sort = "interestingness-desc";
$info_url .= '&api_key=' .$api_key;
$info_url .= '&text=' .$text;
$info_url .= '&sort=' .$sort;
$info_url .= '&safe_search=1';
$info_url .= '&format=json';
$info_url .= '&nojsoncallback=1';
```

The use of `.=` allows developers to append data to a variable. In this case we are appending arguments to the variable `$info_url`.

The arguments that we are interested in are `api_key`, `text`, `sort`, `safe_search`, and `format`.

ARGUMENT	MEANING	REQUIRED
api_key	API Key granted by Flickr	Yes
text	String to search on	Yes
sort	The order in which images are returned; there are many options: date-posted-asc, date-posted-desc, date-taken-asc, date-taken-desc, interestingness-desc, interestingness-asc, and relevance	No

cont.

ARGUMENT	MEANING	REQUIRED
safe_search	Filters mature material: 1 for safe, 2 for moderate, 3 for restricted	No
format	Format of returned data: JSON, XML-RPC, SOAP	No

Replace the values in the variables $api_key, $text, and $sort with your particular values. Your code should look like this:

```php
$api_key = "API key here";
$text = "text string here";
$sort = "interestingness-desc[or sort of your choosing]";
$info_url .= '&api_key=' .$api_key;
$info_url .= '&text=' .$text;
$info_url .= '&sort=' .$sort;
$info_url .= '&safe_search=1';
$info_url .= '&format=json';
$info_url .= '&nojsoncallback=1';
```

The next couple of lines harvest the data dictated by the HTTP request URL, decode it, and put it into a nice, usable array:

```php
$raw_data = file_get_contents($info_url);
$data = json_decode($raw_data);
```

Let's view the array by writing a PHP print_r command:

```php
print '<pre>';
print_r ($data);
print '</pre>';
```

When we open the browser we should see something like this:

```
stdClass Object
(
[photos] => stdClass Object
    (
        [page] => 1
        [pages] => 38420
```

```
        [perpage] => 100
        [total] => 3841994
        [photo] => Array
         (
           [0] => stdClass Object
              (
                 [id] => 5988096829
                 [owner] => 21207178@N07
                 [secret] => 19ef1bb3fb
                 [server] => 6147
                 [farm] => 7
                 [title] => Green Lines planted for Health
                 [ispublic] => 1
                 [isfriend] => 0
                 [isfamily] => 0
              )
           [ . . . ]
```

Something is missing here, isn't it? There's no image, not even a link or a file name. There is one extra step we need to take to display the images. Flickr has standard file paths for all images. For thumbnails, the URL is

```
http://farm'.$farmId.'.static.flickr.com/'.$serverId.'/'.$id.'_'.$secret.'
    _s.jpg
```

And for large images, the URL is

```
http://farm'.$farmId.'.static.flickr.com/'.$serverId.'/'.$id.'_'.$secret.'
    _b.jpg
```

We just need to construct these file paths while including the data from the above array:

```
$images = $data->photos->photo;
if(count($images) > 0) {
```

This bit looks at the results of the query and does the following bit of code only if there are results.

```
echo '<ul>';
```

This creates an unordered HTML list.

```
foreach($images as $image) {
```

21

And this says for every image result in the array, do the following:

```
$farmId = $image->farm;
$serverId = $image->server;
$id = $image->id;
$secret = $image->secret;
$imagePathThumbnail = 'http://farm'.$farmId.'.static.flickr.com/'.$server
      Id.'/'.$id.'_'.$secret.'_s.jpg';
$imagePathLarge = 'http://farm'.$farmId.'.static.flickr.com/'.$serverId.'
      /'.$id.'_'.$secret.'_b.jpg';
```

As you can see, `$imagePathThumbnail` will now include the `$farmId` and `$serverId` of the images in the result set.

Now let's create an image that links out to the original Flickr image as a list item for the already created unordered list:

```
$link = '<li>';
$link .= '<a href="'.$imagePathLarge.'" target="_blank">';
$link .= '<img src="'.$imagePathThumbnail.'" alt="'.$title.'">';
$link .= '</a>';
$link .= '</li>';
echo $link;
}
```

Finally, some finishing touches:

```
echo '</ul>';
}
else {
   echo 'No Results';
}
```

Upon launching the browser, you should see a list of thumbnail-size images that link out to larger versions of the images. Bravo!

In most cases, libraries will be developing web-based applications. Developers can obtain a Flickr API key here: www.flickr.com/services/apps/create/apply.

FLICKR API IN ACTION

The Miami University Libraries embarked upon a Flickr project in the fall of 2009. This API in Action section will delineate how to upload XML files of metadata and images to your Flickr account via the Upload API.

The workflow involves four primary elements:

- The API key and secret code
- Image folder: a local public web directory where all images should be stored
- The XML file: a file based on the Flickr XML template that includes all desired metadata (image filenames must match the filenames in the image folder)
- PHP scripts: required to establish and validate connectivity and parse the XML file into Flickr[4]

All of the files and scripts you will need for this API in Action section can be downloaded here: http://beta.lib.muohio.edu/~jpmichel/flickr_test/flickr _uploader.tar.

API Key

Before you begin the process you will need to obtain an API key and secret code. Go to www.flickr.com/services/api/misc.api_keys.html to begin the process. You will need to give the application a name of your choosing. Next, select "Web Application" as the app type. Finally, enter the URL to auth.php, the authentication script included in the suite of scripts. Be sure to save your API key and secret code, as you will need them later in the process.

The Images

Create a public web directory entitled `flickr_uploader`. In this directory, create a subdirectory entitled `images`. You will place your images for the upload process in this directory. Nothing should be in this directory except the image files.

The XML File

Users have the ability to add text and basic HTML code that describes an image in the description section of each image on Flickr's interface. We decided to include the Subject (TGM) terms and create a hyperlink of the reference URL that links back directly to the corresponding image in our local CONTENTdm collection. Additionally, because the Subject (TGM) field contained a list of terms from a controlled vocabulary, and these were often used to find and browse similar items, we decided to use them as separate tags in Flickr. In the tag element, we also added some new metadata at the collection level—i.e., Miami Digital Collections.

Example of a Flickr XML format

```
<?xml version="1.0" encoding="utf-8"?>
<collection>
 <record>
    <title>Miami women's basketball team 1907</title>
    <description>
    Subject (TGM): Sports; Universities and colleges; Women's education;
    Basketball players; Basketball uniforms; Coaches (Athletics);
    Group portraits;
    Persistent URL: http://digital.lib.muohio.edu/u?/snyder,4215
    </description>
    <tags>
    Sports; Universities and colleges; Women's education;
    Basketball players; Basketball uniforms; Coaches (Athletics);
    Group portraits; Miami Digital Collections
    </tags>
    <file>2063842134.jpg</file>
 </record>
</collection>
```

Converting XML files to Flickr's Required Format

Most digital management systems provide ways to export metadata. In this case, we used the tab-delimited option in CONTENTdm. Ideally, we would have exported an XML file; however, in version 4.3 only the filename was exported using the tab-delimited option. Once the metadata (export.txt) file is in place, follow these steps:

- Open this file (in MS Excel) and select fields with meaningful data—e.g., Title, Subject (TGM).
- Perform a quality-control check of filenames against the actual images.
- Save a new file with only selected fields.
- Run a PHP script that transforms the tab-delimited file into the new Flickr XML format (PHP conversion script available here: http://adler.lib .muohio.edu/~tzocea/files/flickr/).

This is where we created an XML `<record>` element for every image. The title remained the same; the major change was in the `<description>` element. Here we decided to include the data from Subject (TGM) and URL—if we needed to include all the metadata fields, we would have added them here. The next element, `<tags>`, contains the data from Subject (TGM), but Flickr will handle each keyword as a separate tag; this is where we added some new tags at the collection level. Finally, we had the `<file>` element, which should match the image file names.

PHP Scripts

There have been many API kits designed using different programming languages. The class that we used for this process was phpFlickr, written by Dan Coulter. Working with this class our upload script does the following:

- Determines the authenticity of the API key and secret code
- Creates a connection between your data and Flickr's database infrastructure
- Works iteratively through and uploads your images and metadata stored in the XML file to the Flickr profile to which you are logged in

In order to complete this process for your collection, you will only need to edit two PHP files. First, you will enter your API key and secret code into line 11 of upload.php, and then you will do the same into lines 9 and 10 of auth.php. Once your images and XML file are in place, you just need to point your browser to upload.php and the upload process will begin.

NOTES

1. As of June 2012, Flickr ranked 47th on Alexa's global list of the top 500 sites. See www .alexa.com/topsites.
2. "For the Common Good: The Library of Congress Flickr Pilot Project," Library of Congress, October 30, 2008, www.loc.gov/rr/print/flickr_report_final.pdf.
3. For a list of possible arguments, and for more on this Flickr API, go to www.flickr.com/ services/api/flickr.photos.search.html.
4. The upload process could be done in any web programming language.

CHAPTER THREE

VIMEO API AND LIBRARIES

DESIGNING A LIBRARY TUTORIAL VIDEO GALLERY USING VIMEO'S SIMPLE API

Over the past year the Miami University Libraries have been producing videos as a communication vehicle for instruction, outreach, and marketing. To date we have produced nearly thirty videos. In the meantime, the Web Development team was redesigning the library website and hadn't created a space for the videos to live. In the absence of formal place on the website, the videos were hosted at a number of other sites, including Blackboard, Vimeo.com, and iTunes U.

The redesign of the Miami University Libraries' website was accomplished using the Drupal content management system. The developers looked into video-hosting solutions using custom Drupal modules, but in the end it was deemed that the most cost-effective way to host videos on the new website would be to utilize Vimeo's Simple API.

Using Vimeo's API, developers created a number of dynamically generated views for their library video content: a thumbnail gallery view, a list view, and an individual video view. Once the scripts were in place, maintenance of the site was minimal. It was no longer necessary to manually upload all of the videos and descriptions to the site. Once uploaded to Vimeo.com, they are automatically pushed to the library site.

Why Vimeo?

There are wonderful advantages to hosting your videos with other web services. First, it exposes your content to a much wider audience. This is especially useful if that content is valuable to more than just your user base—as we saw in the last chapter with the example of the Library of Congress's historical images on Flickr.

Additionally, by taking advantage of web services and hosting from the cloud, you free up server space and save developer time. There is no time, nor is it any longer necessary, to re-create any wheels. Vimeo.com handles video content well, and it provides its users and developers with a robust, intuitive API to allow for efficient and tailored development.

In addition to the API, Vimeo has strong organizational features. Users are able to create separate, subject-specific albums. For instance, we created an album for video tutorials and for workshop tutorials. As on most social sites, users are also able to apply tags to their videos. The ability to create albums and apply tags is an important tool when developing using the Vimeo API, because you can call up certain videos based on criteria that you specify.

The API data structure is robust and allows for designers to be flexible and creative with their programming.

How the Simple API Works

You can access Vimeo's API through a simple URL request. Using these URL requests you can access and manipulate a wide range of data in three formats: PHP, JSON, and XML.

Let's take a look at a sample URL request:

```
http://vimeo.com/api/v2/miamiulibraries/videos.json
```

Put simply, I requested a list of data in JSON format about all of the videos produced by the user `miamiulibraries`. The first editable piece of the URL after `../v2/` is the type of request you are interested in. You can make requests of individual users, specific videos, groups, channels, and albums.

For example, you could request "info" for a specific user that allows you to see the number of videos produced, number of contacts, display name, URLs of videos, and more. Or you could request "albums," "channels," or "groups" to see information on the different albums or channels the user has created or what groups the user belongs to.

Finally, you add the format of the returned data.

This is an example of the first record in the raw data array that is returned from this request:

```
[{
"id":"9710118","title":"Using Print and Web Resources for Advertising Insight",
description":"",
"url":"http:\/\/vimeo.com\/9710118",
"upload_date":"2010-02-24 14:33:55",
"thumbnail_small":"http:\/\/ts.vimeo.com.s3.amazonaws.
        com\/488\/499\/48849956_100.jpg",
"thumbnail_medium":"http:\/\/ts.vimeo.com.s3.amazonaws.
        com\/488\/499\/48849956_200.jpg",
"thumbnail_large":"http:\/\/ts.vimeo.com.s3.amazonaws.
        com\/488\/499\/48849956_640.jpg",
"user_name":"Miami U. Libraries",
"user_url":"http:\/\/vimeo.com\/miamiulibraries",
"user_portrait_small":"http:\/\/ps.vimeo.com.s3.amazonaws.com\/398\/39829_30
        .jpg",
"user_portrait_medium":"http:\/\/ps.vimeo.com.s3.amazonaws.com\/398\/39829_75
        .jpg",
"user_portrait_large":"http:\/\/ps.vimeo.com.s3.amazonaws.com\/398\/39829_100
        .jpg",
"user_portrait_huge":"http:\/\/ps.vimeo.com.s3.amazonaws.com\/398\/39829_300
        .jpg",
"stats_number_of_likes":"0",
"stats_number_of_plays":"1",
"stats_number_of_comments":"0",
"duration":"290",
"width":"640",
"height":"480",
"tags":""
}]
```

You can see that Vimeo offers a lot of data through its API and will therefore allow for many different options when it comes to displaying the data.

How We Used the API

We used Vimeo's Simple API to create three gallery views: one for all videos, one for all videos in our "workshop" album, and one for all videos in our "tutorial" album. We also allowed for an individual video view and two menu views.

The primary view displays all of the videos in tabular format with a thumbnail screenshot of each video and the title, both of which link to that individual video. Above this tabular listing of all videos is a "featured" video that includes the title and description of the video as well as the video itself in an embedded Flash player. This featured video is randomized and will be different each time the page loads.

Here is the script used to create this gallery view with a randomized featured video:

```
$info_url = "http://vimeo.com/api/v2/miamiulibraries/videos.json";
//this is the Vimeo API call, which grabs data on all of the videos produced by
      our account //"miamiulibraries"
 $raw_data = file_get_contents($info_url);
//transforms the raw data into a string
 $data = json_decode($raw_data);
//decodes the json string and turns it into a PHP variable
 $count = count($data);
//counts the number of videos
 $rand = rand(1,$count);
//produces a random number to use to display the random featured video
 $columns = 5;
    $video = $data[$rand];
    print '<p><strong>View: </strong><a href="/workshop_videos">Workshop
       Videos</a> | <a href="/tutorial_videos">Tutorial Videos</a> | <a href="/
       videos">All Videos</a></p>';
    print '<div style="border: 2px solid #cccccc; background-color: #efefef;">
    <table border="0" bgcolor="#efefef">
    <tr>
    <td>
    <object width="400" height="300">
    <param name="allowfullscreen" value="true" />
    <param name="allowscriptaccess" value="always" />
    <param name="movie" value="http://vimeo.com/moogaloop.swf?clip_id='. $video
       ->id .'&amp;server=vimeo.com&amp;show_title=1&amp;show_byline=1&amp;show_
       portrait=0&amp;color=&amp;fullscreen=1" />
//URL calls up the Flash file of the video based on calling the video ID element
      in the array ($video->id)
    <embed src="http://vimeo.com/moogaloop.swf?clip_id='. $video->id
       .'&amp;server=vimeo.com&amp;show_title=1&amp;show_byline=1&amp;show_port
       rait=0&amp;color=&amp;fullscreen=1" type="application/x-shockwave-flash"
       allowfullscreen="true" allowscriptaccess="always" border="1" width="400"
       height="300">
    </embed>
    </object>
//embeds the Vimeo Flash player
    </td>
    <td width="400" valign="top">
    <h1 class="in_node">Featured Video</h1><h3 class="in_node"><a href="http://
       vimeo.com/'. $video->id .'">'. $video->title .'</a></h3> from <a href="'
       . $video->user_url .'">'. $video->user_name. '</a> on <a href="http://
       vimeo.com">Vimeo</a>
    <br /><br />
//inserts title of video ($video->title) in link to the video ($video->id) and
      the user ($video->user_url) //at vimeo.com
```

```
      <div style="border-top: 2px solid #cccccc;"><p>'. $video->description .'
         </p></div>
      </td>
      </tr>
      </table>
      </div>
      <br />';
   print '<div style="border-top: 1px solid #3399cc;"><table border="0"><tr>';
      for ($i = 0; $i < $count; $i++){
         $video = $data[$i];
         if ( !($i % $columns) && $i) {
          $output .= '</tr><tr>';
         }
         $output .= '<td><h4><a href="/selected_video?videoId='. $video->id .'">'
            . $video->title .'</a></h4><a href="/selected_video?videoId= '. $video
            ->id .'"><img src="'. $video->thumbnail_small .'"></a></td>';
      }
   print '</tr></table></div>';
   //outputs row of five records each with a thumbnail and title linking to
      individual video view
```

We used the same script to output a gallery view for our "Tutorial" album and "Workshop" album.

The individual video view displays the title and description of the video as well as the video itself in the embedded Vimeo Flash player.

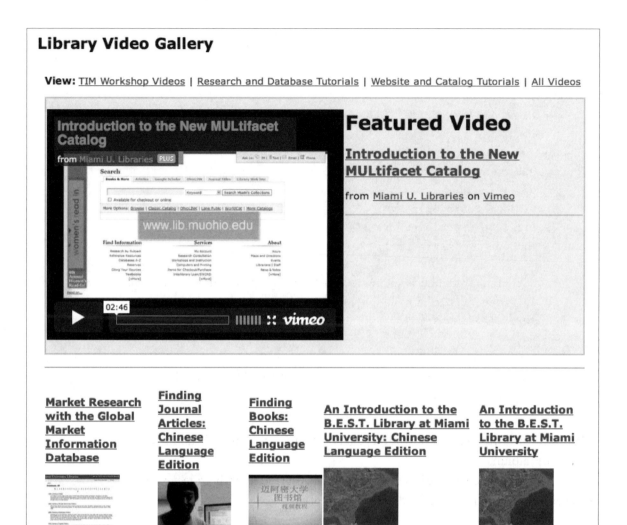

Here is the script used to create a view of a selected video:

```php
$videoId = $_GET['videoId'];
//grabs the video ID as passed through the referring URL
$info_url = "http://vimeo.com/api/v2/video/$videoId.json";
//the URL to request data from one particular video in JSON format
$raw_data = file_get_contents($info_url);
//transforms the raw data into a string
$data = json_decode($raw_data);
//decodes the JSON string and turns it into a PHP variable
for ($i = 0; $i >= 0; $i--){
$video = $data[$i];
print "<table border="0">
    <tr>
    <td>
    <object width="400" height="300">
```

```
            <param name="allowfullscreen" value="true" />
            <param name="allowscriptaccess" value="always" />
<param name="movie" value="http://vimeo.com/moogaloop.swf?clip_id='. $video->id
        .'&amp;server=vimeo.com&amp;show_title=1&amp;show_byline=1&amp;show_portr
        ait=0&amp;color=&amp;fullscreen=1" />
//URL calls up the Flash file of the video based on calling the video ID element
        in the array ($video->id)
<embed src="http://vimeo.com/moogaloop.swf?clip_id='. $video->id
        .'&amp;server=vimeo.com&amp;show_title=1&amp;show_byline=1&amp;show_port
        rait=0&amp;color=&amp;fullscreen=1" type="application/x-shockwave-flash"
        allowfullscreen="true" allowscriptaccess="always" border="1" width="400"
        height="300">
            </embed>
            </object>
            </td>
            <td>
            <h3 class="in_node"><a href="http://vimeo.com/'. $video->id .'">'. $video
                ->title .'</a></h3> from <a href="'. $video->user_url .'">'. $video
                ->user_name. '</a> on <a href="http://vimeo.com">Vimeo</a>
//inserts title of video ($video->title) in link to the video ($video->id) and
        the user ($video->user_url) //at vimeo.com
            </td>
            </tr>
            </table>";
print "<p>'. $video->description .'</p>
//prints the description of the video
        <p><strong>Back to: </strong><a href="http://dev.lib.muohio.edu:8082
            /workshop_videos">Workshop Videos</a> | <a href="http://dev.lib.muohio
            .edu:8082/tutorial_videos">Tutorial Videos</a> | <a href="http://dev.lib
            .muohio.edu:8082/videos">All Videos</a>";
```

CHAPTER FOUR

GOOGLE CHARTS API AND LIBRARIES

For the uninitiated, Google Charts may seem like an odd choice to include in this book. But once you explore the service and consider the importance of data visualization, you'll see that Google Charts is an invaluable service in today's information environment.

Google Charts offers several data visualization schemes, all coded in HTML5, that require no plugins. Options include pie charts, scatter charts, gauges, geographic charts, tables, tree maps, combo charts, line charts, bar charts, column charts, area charts, candlestick charts, and more. Google Charts also provides QR codes, dynamic icons, and other infographic tools.

There are a number of promising applications for libraries using Google Charts. Be aware, however, that for some of them you'll need access to your library's data, which isn't always possible depending on the ILS you are using.

QR Codes

If your library has a mobile site, QR codes can be a valuable technology. Libraries can embed QR codes in bibliographic description pages that send location information to a user's mobile device or direct a user to similar materials on your mobile site. Or, QR codes affixed to individual books can link to other mobilized content related to that book, such as books by the same author, books on the same subject, articles on the same subject, and more.

Statistical Data Visualization

From a management perspective, statistics have always been an important factor in the decision-making process. Using Google Charts to present this data can potentially lead to better decisions. Types of data that can take advantage of Google Charts: circulation statistics, door counts, computer usage, and more.

Resource Availability Visualization

Many libraries are becoming known for their technology and space resources in addition to their collections. Because of this, it is increasingly important to provide information to patrons as to the availability of these resources. Google Charts can provide the visualization tools to present the availability of resources such as study rooms and computers.

GOOGLE CHARTS API TECHNICAL DETAILS

Google Charts API Overview

The Google Charts API works very much like the other APIs discussed in this book, operating via URL GET or POST requests.

The base URL for the Google Charts API is

```
https://chart.googleapis.com/chart?
```

This URL is then followed by multiple parameters determining the type, data, and layout of the chart. Each chart type has a set of specific parameters. For a list of all parameters go here: http://code.google.com/apis/chart/image/docs/chart_params.html.

Let's get started with a small example illustrating how Google Charts could be used to display computer usage and availability with a pie chart. For this example, let's assume you have access to real-time computer usage statistics.

After the base URL of `https://chart.googleapis.com/chart?` let's append our parameters. The parameters we will be using for this example are as follows:

PARAMETER	VALUES	USAGE
cht	Predetermined code; pie chart is p3	Determines the chart type
chs	Width and height; in pixels	Determines the chart size
chd	Depends on available statistics; for this example, t: 18, 82	Chart data
chl	Labels corresponding with data numbers	Slice labels

Let's create a pie chart indicating that currently 18 percent of our computers are available.

The URL will look like this:

```
https://chart.googleapis.com/chart?cht=p3&chs=400x150&chd=t:18,82&chco=4CC417,
     FF0000&chl=18|82
```

This URL will return a pie chart indicating that 18 percent of the computers are available and 82 percent are not available.

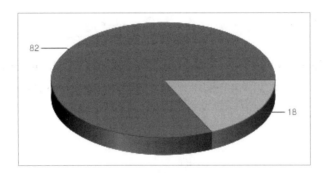

This pie chart API would work equally well with resources such as study rooms and laptop and other equipment checkouts.

GOOGLE CHARTS API IN ACTION

Let's expand on the concept above to produce an application that records laptop checkouts and then, utilizing the Google Charts API, displays a pie chart indicating availability. The PHP scripts we will write will both construct the appropriate Google Charts URL and display the data.

This is a very simple example that you could expand into a viable service for the benefit of patrons.

To begin, we need to create a simple database table. In this example, we will use MySQL, but you can use any other database tool you are comfortable with as long as it interacts properly with PHP.

This simple table has two fields: laptop name (name) and Boolean availability of laptops (avail).

Enter the following MySQL command to create the table laptops:

```
CREATE TABLE laptops (id INT NOT NULL AUTO_INCREMENT, name VARCHAR(30), avail
        BOOL, PRIMARY KEY(id));
```

Let's fill this table with some initial data:

```
INSERT INTO laptops (name, avail) VALUES ('Laptop A', 1);
```

Continue entering data into your table using any naming convention you'd like. For this example, the laptops will be called Laptop A, B, C, etc. The avail value 1 means the laptop is available.

Now that we have a database table to record the status of our laptops, we need a simple web-based interface to allow administrators to do so. To do that, we will create a simple HTML form which then inserts that form data into the MySQL database via PHP.

```
<?php
print '<form action="laptop_status.php" method="get">
```

Here we begin the form, and as you can see the data obtained in the form will be sent to laptop_status.php—which we will write in a moment. Let's continue the form:

```
<ul>
<li>Laptop A</li>
<ul>
<li><input type="radio" name="laptopa" value="1" />Available<br />
<input type="radio" name="laptopa" value="0" />Not Available<br /></li>
</ul>
<li>Laptop B</li>
. . .
</ul>
<input type="submit" value="Submit" />
</form>';
```

The web-based form when rendered will look like this:

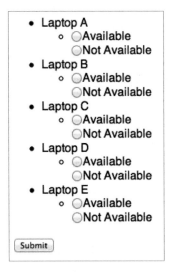

The next piece to this application is a PHP script that will take the submitted data from the above form and insert it into the MySQL table `laptops`:

```php
<?php
$con = mysql_connect("localhost","db_user","password");
```

Open up a data stream between PHP script and MySQL. The parameters `db_user` and `password` will be replaced with your specifics.

```php
if (!$con)
{
    die('Could not connect: ' . mysql_error( ));
}
```

This is a debugging function. If no MySQL connection is made you will receive a MySQL error message. Next we select the proper database using the credentials stored in the variable `$con`:

```php
else {
mysql_select_db("db_name", $con);
```

Now for the heart of the matter. Here we update the `laptops` table with the availability status values submitted via the HTML form:

```
mysql_query("UPDATE laptops SET avail = '$_GET[laptopa]' WHERE name =
    'Laptop A'");
mysql_query("UPDATE laptops SET avail = '$_GET[laptopb]' WHERE name =
    'Laptop B'");
mysql_query("UPDATE laptops SET avail = '$_GET[laptopc]' WHERE name =
    'Laptop C'");
mysql_query("UPDATE laptops SET avail = '$_GET[laptopd]' WHERE name =
    'Laptop D'");
mysql_query("UPDATE laptops SET avail = '$_GET[laptope]' WHERE name =
    'Laptop E'");
mysql_close($con);
}
?>
```

Now we have a dynamic database that records in real time the availability of laptops. To inform patrons of this availability, we need to finish this application with a PHP script that constructs the Google Charts API URL and displays the data:

```
<?php
$con = mysql_connect("localhost","jpmichel","pencil");
if (!$con)
{
    die('Could not connect: ' . mysql_error( ));
}
    else {
        mysql_select_db("jpmichel", $con);
```

Now that we've made our connection with the database table, we will begin to create variables that we will use to construct our URL request. Here we have very simple variables that tell us how many database entries, or laptops, have an availability status of 1 or 0:

```
$data1 = mysql_query("select count(*) from laptops where avail = 1");
$data2 = mysql_query("select count(*) from laptops where avail = 0");
```

Since `$data1` and `$data2` are arrays, we need to process the data a bit more using the `mysql_fetch_array` function to create the usable variables of `$avail` and `$not_avail`, which will be rendered in arabic numerals:

```
$avail = mysql_fetch_array($data1);
$not_avail = mysql_fetch_array($data2);
}
```

Finally, we can construct the URL request in the form on an embedded image:

```
print '<img src="https://chart.googleapis.com/chart?cht=p3&chs=400x150&chd=t:'
      . $avail[0] .','. $not_avail[0] .'&chco=4CC417,FF0000&chl='. $avail[0] .'
      are available|'. $not_avail[0] .' are not available" />';
?>
```

Let's break down the URL a bit.
First we've got the default Google Charts API URL:

```
https://chart.googleapis.com/chart?
```

What follows are the parameters that will determine the final look of the chart:

```
cht=p3&chs=400x150
```

From what we've learned earlier, this section tells Google to return a 400x150 pixel pie chart.

```
&chd=t:'. $avail[0] .','. $not_avail[0] .'
```

Here is the spot in the URL request where we insert data from our database. The values for `$avail[0]` and `$not_avail[0]` will be returned in arabic numerals.

```
&chco=4CC417,FF0000&chl='. $avail[0] .' are available|'. $not_avail[0] .' are
      not available
```

The final touches: `chco` indicates the HTML colors used to indicate availability status and `chl` indicates labels used on the chart.

When this PHP script is rendered in a browser, you should see something like this:

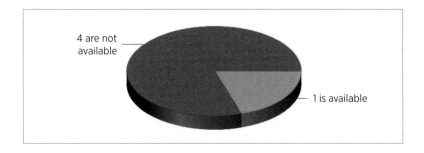

SPOTLIGHT ON MONTANA STATE UNIVERSITY LIBRARIES

Two librarians at Montana State University Libraries, Jason Clark and Tim Donahue, built an application that dynamically outputs a QR code with encoded vCard data related to each staff member on their profile pages.[1] When the QR code is scanned, the staff member's contact information is automatically added to the mobile device's contact list. They achieved this through the use of the Google Charts API.

The application consists of a MySQL database, similar to what we described above, and a PHP script hooking into the Google Charts API.

GOOGLE CHARTS QR CODE EXAMPLES

The Miami University Libraries use the Google Charts API to display a QR code in the full record view of each book in the catalog. When scanned, the QR code displays the title and location of the book. This is a good option for users to quickly get the location information on their phones without writing it down or entering their phone number to have it sent via SMS.

Let's build a little script that dynamically generates QR codes with book location information encoded.

The Google Charts QR code API is very simple. The only piece of data that the URL request returns is the QR code itself. The base URL is

```
https://chart.googleapis.com/chart?
```

As with our previous example we need to add a few parameters to this base string. One is the chart size, or `chs`:

```
https://chart.googleapis.com/chart?chs=150x150
```

The next parameter is chart type, or `cht`:

```
https://chart.googleapis.com/chart?chs=150x150&cht=qr
```

Finally, we need to add the URL encoded data, or `chl`:

```
https://chart.googleapis.com/chart?chs=150x150&cht=qr&chl=The+Sound+and+the+Fury
    +%7C+King+Library+%7C+PN355+.F8
```

Take this URL and enter it into your browser. What is returned is a QR code with the following encoded string: The Sound and the Fury | King Library | PN355 .F8.
Let's write up a script that returns this QR code:

```php
<?php
$data = urlencode("The Sound and the Fury | King Library | PN355 .F8");
```

This variable is the string that we want to be embedded in the QR code. In a real situation this string will be dynamically generated with data from the catalog. It must be URL encoded.

```php
$url = "https://chart.googleapis.com/chart?chs=150x150&cht=qr";
```

That's our base URL request string, to which we append the following additions:

```php
$url .= "&chl=";
$url .= "$data";
```

Ensure that the URL is constructed properly by using the echo function:

```php
echo $url;
```

Upon opening up the browser you should see:

> https://chart.googleapis.com/chart?chs=150x150&cht=qr&chl=The+Sound+and+the+Fury+%7C+King+Library+%7C+PN355+.F8

To test whether or not the URL is properly constructed, copy what is echoed out to the screen and paste it in the URL bar. If a QR code is returned then it's correct. Go ahead and either delete or comment out the echo line:

```php
//echo $url;
```

Now all we need to do is print out the QR code as an image, using the URL as the src:

```php
print '<img src="' . $url . '" />';
?>
```

Save the file and open it in your browser. What you should see now is the QR code that when scanned reads

The Sound and the Fury | King Library | PN355 .F8

Here's the full script:

```php
<?php
$data = urlencode("The Sound and the Fury | King Library | PN355 .F8");
$url = "https://chart.googleapis.com/chart?chs=150x150&cht=qr";
$url .= "&chl=";
$url .= "$data";
echo $url;
print '<img src="' . $url . '" />';
?>
```

NOTE

1.   "QR Codes in Action!," www.lib.montana.edu/~jason/talks/il2011-qr-codes-action.pdf.

CHAPTER FIVE

OCLC WEB SERVICES AND LIBRARIES

OCLC, the world's largest library cooperative, provides an impressive suite of web service APIs for developers to utilize. These APIs provide access to OCLC's wide variety of library data and services that have been built up over decades of work by librarians and library administrators across the country and the world. OCLC's primary tools are as follows:

- **WorldCat Search API.** Provides full-scale access to WorldCat's bibliographic data and library holdings.
- **WorldCat Basic API.** A scaled-down version of the WorldCat Search API. Returns bibliographic data on WorldCat's holdings. We will discuss this API in detail.
- **WorldCat Registry.** A central portal for institutional data about libraries. Includes services that allow libraries to share their data with vendors and others. See www.oclc.org/registry/default.htm.
- **xISBN.** Returns ISBNs related to a specific ISBN. Useful for displaying other editions of a work. We will discuss and work with this API later in this chapter.
- **xISSN.** Returns related ISSNs and history of a serial. Useful for displaying previous and subsequent titles of a particular journal. We will discuss and work with this API later in this chapter.

WORLDCAT BASIC API TECHNICAL DETAILS

The WorldCat Basic API is a scaled-down version of the WorldCat Search API and is thus a useful introduction to OCLC's web services. The API returns basic bibliographic information, including citations, for books, videos, music, and other holdings in the WorldCat catalog.

The API runs on the OpenSearch query protocol and is limited to 1,000 requests per day. The results are returned in either RSS or Atom format, making it different from most of the APIs we've covered thus far in the book. Because of this, we will introduce another element to our PHP scripts, cURL, which will help to parse the returned data.

Before working with the WorldCat Basic API you will need to obtain a developer key at https://worldcat.org/config. The developer key will be used as the `wskey` parameter in the OpenSearch URL request.

To get started and to see the raw data that is returned, enter the following URL in your browser:

```
http://worldcat.org/webservices/catalog/search/worldcat/opensearch?q=[query
      -text]&start=1&count=50&cformat=MLA&format=atom&wskey=your_key
```

What you should see returned is an Atom XML feed that looks like this:

```
<?xml version="1.0" encoding="UTF-8" standalone="no"?>
<feed xmlns="http://www.w3.org/2005/Atom" xmlns:xsi="http://www.w3.org/2001
      /XMLSchema-instance" xmlns:diag="http://www.loc.gov/zing/srw/diagnostic/"
      xmlns:oclcterms="http://purl.org/oclc/terms/" xmlns:dc="http://purl.org
      /dc/elements/1.1/" xmlns:opensearch="http://a9.com/-/spec/opensearch
      /1.1/">
<title>OCLC Worldcat Search: dissent</title>
<id>http://worldcat.org/webservices/catalog/search/worldcat/opensearch?q=
      dissent&amp;start=1&amp;count=50&amp;cformat=MLA&amp;format=atom&amp;wske
      y=[parameter-key]</id>
<updated>2011-11-27T18:56:57-05:00</updated>
<subtitle>Search results for dissent at http://worldcat.org/webservices
      /catalog</subtitle>
<opensearch:totalResults>12365</opensearch:totalResults>
<opensearch:startIndex>1</opensearch:startIndex>
<opensearch:itemsPerPage>50</opensearch:itemsPerPage>
<opensearch:Query role="request" searchTerms="dissent" startPage="1"/>
...
<link rel="search" type="application/opensearchdescription+xml" href="http://
      worldcat.org/webservices/catalog/opensearch.description.xml"/>
<entry>
   <author>
      <name>Young, Alfred Fabian, 1925- comp.</name>
   </author>
```

```
    <title>Dissent</title>
    <link href="http://worldcat.org/oclc/421327"/>
    <id>http://worldcat.org/oclc/421327</id>
    <updated>2011-01-15T02:43:36Z</updated>
    <content type="html">&lt;p class="citation_style_MLA"&gt;Young, Alfred F.
        &lt;i&gt;Dissent&lt;/i&gt;. DeKalb: Northern Illinois University Press,
        1968. Print. &lt;/p&gt;</content>
    <dc:identifier>urn:ISBN:0875800076</dc:identifier>
    <dc:identifier>urn:ISBN:9780875800073</dc:identifier>
    <dc:identifier>urn:ISBN:0875805027</dc:identifier>
    <dc:identifier>urn:ISBN:9780875805023</dc:identifier>
    <dc:identifier>urn:LCCN:68057389</dc:identifier>
    <oclcterms:recordIdentifier>421327</oclcterms:recordIdentifier>
</entry>
```

There will undoubtedly be additional `<entry>` items after the initial entry, but you can see the type of data with which you have to work. Primarily you will have titles, authors, citations, and links to the WorldCat entries.

Let's break down this URL to get a quick handle on the parameters and how you may utilize them.

```
http://worldcat.org/webservices/catalog/search/worldcat/opensearch?
```

This is the trunk of the request URL. The parameters will follow this.

PARAMETER	MEANING	REQUIRED
q	Search query	Yes
start	Start position of returned data	No; if left out will default to position 1
count	Number of returned records	No; if left out will default to a count of 10
format	Format of data returned; RSS or Atom	No; if left out will default to Atom
cformat	Format of citations; supported styles are APA, Chicago, Harvard, MLA, and Turabian	No
wskey	Developer key	Yes

Let's continue building the URL:

```
http://worldcat.org/webservices/catalog/search/worldcat
     /opensearch?q=API&wskey=your_key
```

When entered in a browser this URL returns a list of ten entries in Atom XML format, starting at position one without a formatted citation.

Let's add a starting position and see what we get:

```
http://worldcat.org/webservices/catalog/search/worldcat/opensearch?q=API&start=
     10&wskey=your_key
```

If you chose a start position of 10, the last entry in your previous set of results should now be in position 1.

Now let's return more than ten entries by setting `count` to 100:

```
http://worldcat.org/webservices/catalog/search/worldcat/opensearch?q=API&start=
     10&count=100&wskey=your_key
```

If you'd like to change the default format of the returned XML to RSS, just set `format` to `rss`:

```
http://worldcat.org/webservices/catalog/search/worldcat/opensearch?q=API&start=
     10&count=100&format=rss&wskey=your_key
```

Whether to choose Atom or RSS will depend on the type of application you build and personal preferences.

Finally, we can adjust the citation format that is returned. If you'd like to return a specific style, such as MLA, you can add it to the URL, or you can choose `all` to return all supported citation styles. Many libraries, including Miami University of Ohio, utilize this functionality to give students quick access to all citation styles.

Here's the URL to return all citation styles:

```
http://worldcat.org/webservices/catalog/search/worldcat/opensearch?q=API&start=
     10&count=100&format=rss&cformat=all&wskey=your_key
```

To choose a specific style, merely substitute `all` with your style of choice. Supported styles appear in the table above, under `cformat`.

Now, that we're seeing how the parameters within the URL request are working, let's put this API into an application.

WORLDCAT BASIC API IN ACTION

This section will guide you through a step-by-step process to request, parse, and display WorldCat Basic data. Depending on the openness of your institution's ILS, you could integrate an application like this into your catalog to display additional resources related to a local search or merely provide links to quick citations, as implemented by the Miami University Libraries.

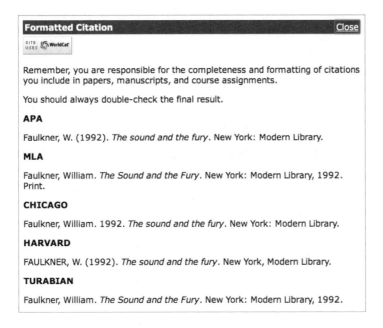

As in the other API in Action sections, this script will be written using PHP. Create a new `.php` file on your local web server. To start the script we will declare the variables of the URL parameters like so:

```php
<?php
$query = urlencode("world war II");
$format = "atom";
$start = "1";
$count = "10";
$cformat = "mla";
$key = "your_key_here";
```

Everything here should be recognizable. The first variable may need a bit of explication. You may recall from earlier chapters that `urlencode` is a PHP function for encoding strings that are intended to be passed as a URL. Strings containing special characters or spaces will need to be encoded in this way or risk not being processed properly by the browser. To test this function out, choose a multiword phrase as the `$query` variable, such as "`world war II`". The query string for this script is being hard-coded by us; however, it is more likely that in a live application this string will be a dynamic value coming from a user search.

We will come back to this a bit later.

Now that we have the necessary URL parameters declared as variables, we can move on to the next step—constructing the URL:

```
$url = "http://worldcat.org/webservices/catalog/search/worldcat/";
$url .= "opensearch?q=".$query;
$url .= "&format=".$format;
$url .= "&start=".$start;
$url .= "&count=".$count;
$url .= "&cformat=".$cformat;
$url .= "&wskey=".$key;
```

What this section is doing is declaring an initial URL variable, being the root URL prior to the parameters. The additional `$url` values are being concatenated to the initial `$url` via the `.=` operator.

Thus, `opensearch?q=` is being added to the end of the root URL; `&format=` is being added after `opensearch?q="query"`, and so on. This method allows developers to change the values in the URL without editing the URL itself.

Now that we have the URL properly structured we can begin the process of extracting the data. An initial step in this process is to massage the returned data with cURL since PHP does not have any built-in functions for handling RSS or Atom data.

Essentially, cURL allows us to retrieve entire web documents, files, and more via the command line. To begin a cURL session:

```
$ch = curl_init($url);
```

We are calling this variable `$ch` because the `curl_init` function returns a cURL handle. `curl_init` initializes a cURL session using the URL declared earlier in the script. This cURL handle will be used in the following steps:

```
curl_setopt($ch, CURLOPT_RETURNTRANSFER, true);
curl_setopt($ch, CURLOPT_HEADER, 0);
```

These two functions here are setting options for the cURL session. The first option, `CURLOPT_RETURNTRANSFER, true`, is essentially telling cURL to save the returned data as a string in the executed cURL session variable, rather than printing it out directly.

The second option being declared, `CURLOPT_HEADER, 0,` is telling cURL to not include the header section of the returned page. The next step is to execute the cURL request:

```
$data = curl_exec($ch);
curl_close($ch);
```

Now we have the returned data stored as a string in `$data`. But this data is in XML format, so we need a couple more steps to allow us to manipulate and output the data in HTML:

```
$doc = new SimpleXmlElement($data, LIBXML_NOCDATA);
$count = count($doc->entry);
```

Before we move on to outputting the data in HTML format, let's take a look at how the data has been changed by the various functions performed on it:

```
print '<pre>';
print_r ($data);
print '</pre>';
```

Open this PHP script in your browser to take a look. What these lines are doing is printing out `$data`, which is the result of the cURL-executed session. Notice that the data does not contain any XML formatting and is merely printed out HTML. That's why we needed to perform the last function:

```
$doc = new SimpleXmlElement($data, LIBXML_NOCDATA);
```

Now try this:

```
print '<pre>';
print_r ($doc);
print '</pre>';
```

You'll notice that this time the data is formatted differently than in its previous iteration. It's been put into an XML format that can then be parsed using PHP. Now all that is left to do is output the HTML with the WorldCat data using a standard DOCTYPE declaration and head section:

```
print '<!DOCTYPE HTML PUBLIC "-//W3C//DTD HTML 4.01 Transitional//EN" "http://
     www.w3.org/TR/html4/loose.dtd">';
print '<html>';
print '<head>
```

```
<meta http-equiv="Content-Type" content="text/html; charset=utf-8">
</head>';
```

Then create a `for` loop to work iteratively through the XML document:

```
print '<body>';
print '<ul>';
for ($i = 0; $i < $count; $i++) {
print '<li><a href=' . $doc->entry[$i]->id . '>' . $doc->entry[$i]->title
    . '</a> by ' . $doc->entry[$i]->author->name . '<br />' . $doc
    ->entry[$i]->content . '</li>';
}
print '</ul>
    </body>';
```

Loading this in the browser should produce something that looks similar to this:

- World War II by Adams, Simon, 1955-

  Adams, Simon. *World War II*. New York: Dorling Kindersley, 2000. Print.
- D-Day, June 6, 1944 : the climactic battle of World War II by Ambrose, Stephen E.

  Ambrose, Stephen E. *D-day, June 6, 1944: The Climactic Battle of World War II*. New York: Simon & Schuster, 1994. Print.
- World War II by Willmott, H. P.

  Willmott, H P, Robin Cross, and Charles Messenger. *World War II*. New York: DK Pub, 2004. Print.
- Unbroken : a World War II story of survival, resilience, and redemption by Hillenbrand, Laura.

  Hillenbrand, Laura. *Unbroken: A World War II Story of Survival, Resilience, and Redemption*. New York: Random House, 2010. Print.
- PT 109 : John F. Kennedy in World War II by Donovan, Robert J.

  Donovan, Robert J. *PT 109: John F. Kennedy in World War II*. New York: McGraw-Hill, 1961. Print.
- Daring missions of World War II by Breuer, William B., 1923-

  Breuer, William B. *Daring Missions of World War II*. New York: Wiley, 2001. Internet resource.
- World War II by Snyder, Louis L. (Louis Leo), 1907-1993.

  Snyder, Louis L. *World War II*. New York: F. Watts, 1981. Print.
- World War II by Time-Life Books.

  World War II. Alexandria, VA: Time-Life Books, 1997. Print.
- World War II by Sulzberger, C. L. (Cyrus Leo), 1912-1993.

  Sulzberger, C L. *World War II*. New York: American Heritage, 1985. Print.

Earlier in this chapter I reintroduced a PHP function called `urlencode` and said I would come back to it. To see the effect `urlencode` has on this script, simply remove it from the variable declaration. Thus, change:

```
$query = urlencode("world war II");
```

to:

```
$query = "world war II";
```

When the script is now run, it throws up an error. Always use `urlencode` when creating variables destined to be passed through URLs.

Here's the complete script:

```php
<?php
$query = urlencode("world war II");
$format = "atom";
$start = "1";
$count = "10";
$cformat = "mla";
$key = "your_key_here";
$url = "http://worldcat.org/webservices/catalog/search/worldcat/";
$url .= "opensearch?q=".$query;
$url .= "&format=".$format;
$url .= "&start=".$start;
$url .= "&count=".$count;
$url .= "&cformat=".$cformat;
$url .= "&wskey=".$key;
$ch = curl_init($url);
curl_setopt($ch, CURLOPT_RETURNTRANSFER, true);
curl_setopt($ch, CURLOPT_HEADER, 0);
$data = curl_exec($ch);
curl_close($ch);
$doc = new SimpleXmlElement($data, LIBXML_NOCDATA);
$count = count($doc->entry);
echo $count;
print '<!DOCTYPE HTML PUBLIC "-//W3C//DTD HTML 4.01 Transitional//EN" "http://
    www.w3.org/TR/html4/loose.dtd">';
print '<html>';
print '<head>
    <meta http-equiv="Content-Type" content="text/html; charset=utf-8">
    </head>';
print '<body>';
print '<ul>';
for ($i = 0; $i < $count; $i++) {
print '<li><a href=' . $doc->entry[$i]->id . '>' . $doc->entry[$i]->title .
    '</a> by ' . $doc->entry[$i]->author->name . '<br />' .
    $doc->entry[$i]->content . '</li>';
}
print '</ul>';
```

```
print '</body>';
print '</html>';
?>
```

WORLDCAT XISBN API

The WorldCat xISBN API can be utilized in conjunction with the WorldCat Basic API to return bibliographic data on related ISBNs. For example, you might write an xISBN script to construct a sidebar or section in your catalog that lists various editions or translations of a particular title based on its ISBN.

This would be a useful service if, for example, a desired title was checked out. The catalog might then display other editions.

What we are going to do is edit the WorldCat Basic API example that we've already scripted. If you haven't done that one yet, then you can pick up with this example.

Essentially, xISBN returns a list of ISBNs related to the submitted ISBN query. The base URL request format for the xISBN service is

```
http://xisbn.worldcat.org/webservices/xid/isbn/
```

There are several parameters for this request:

PARAMETER	MEANING	REQUIRED
isbn	ISBN value	Yes
method	Determines the data the xISBN service will return; getEditions is the default	Yes
format	Format of data returned; supported formats are XML, JSON, CSV, TEXT, Python, Ruby, XHTML	Yes

The xISBN service has several methods to choose from. For a full-featured list of methods, go to http://xisbn.worldcat.org/xisbnadmin/doc/api.htm#request. For this example we will use the default method of getEditions.

If you are editing the script that you put together for the WorldCat Basic API in Action section, append these bits of code to the beginning of the script. Let's get started.

First, we need a value for the variable $xisbn. Here, we are hard-coding it; under real conditions, it is more likely that this variable would be dynamically generated through a catalog search.

```php
<?php
$xisbn = "0553103547";
```

Now let's declare our `method` and `format` parameters. Again, it is best to declare these values as variables rather than hard-coding them.

```php
$xmethod = "getEditions";
$xformat = "json";
```

Now we need our base URL request format:

```php
$xurl ="http://xisbn.worldcat.org/webservices/xid/isbn/$xisbn";
```

And then we need to concatenate our `method` and `format` parameters to the base URL:

```php
$xurl .= "?method=$xmethod";
$xurl .= "&format=$xformat";
```

This is why it is best to declare your values as variables. You can then more readily change the method and format to suit your needs.

At this point, you can echo out your $xurl to verify that the script is indeed constructing it properly:

```php
echo $xurl;
```

Point your browser to this URL and take a look.

Now it's time to get the data, which again is a list of ISBNs related to the original ISBN:

```php
$xraw_data = file_get_contents($xurl);
```

Echo out this variable to see the type of data being returned:

```php
echo $xraw_data;
```

As you can see, there is a JSON string being returned. We will need to decode the JSON before working with it. On a side note, when scripting, it is useful to use the `echo` function on some of your variables on occasion to see what you are working with. You can then either leave that function in or comment the line out by using `//`. This is good for debugging.

Now let's take the JSON-encoded data within `$xraw_data` and convert it to a PHP variable—i.e., `$xdata` that we can manipulate:

```
$xdata = json_decode($xraw_data);
```

To look at the architecture of `$xdata`, we will need to employ a separate PHP function called `print_r`. This is just a way of printing or echoing out the data, but it is formatted and structured in a more readable way:

```
print '<pre>';
print_r ($xdata);
print '</pre>';
```

After you've taken a look at `$xdata`, go ahead and comment out the above lines. To continue with the script:

```
$xcount = count ($xdata->list);
```

Now that we have our list of ISBNs in a PHP object, we can move on to the World-Cat Basic API portion of this script. It varies a bit from the script we put together for the WorldCat Basic API in Action section.

The next step is to set the DOCTYPE declaration and HTML head information:

```
print '<!DOCTYPE HTML PUBLIC "-//W3C//DTD HTML 4.01 Transitional//EN" "http://
     www.w3.org/TR/html4/loose.dtd">';
print '<html>';
print '<head>
  <meta http-equiv="Content-Type" content="text/html; charset=utf-8">
  </head>';
```

Next, we will start an unordered list:

```
print '<ul>';
```

What we are putting together is a list of items that are returned from the World-Cat Basic API, based on a list of ISBNs pulled from xISBN. Congratulations, you are scripting using two APIs in one!

Now for our `for` loop declaration:

```
for ($i = 0; $i < $xcount; $i++) {
```

This is saying for each ISBN encountered do the following:

```
$query = $xdata->list[$i]->isbn[0];
```

So, essentially, each ISBN is being turned into a `query` parameter for the WorldCat Basic API.

Continuing with the `for` loop:

```
$start = "1";
$count = "10";
$cformat = "mla";
$key = "6mmkTZ1LSocFfDIXYi0871UiaM4Unh6SuguN2HmAq9FvsFBn8Elr7rMhs09UvoJUpxhXfUap
      Q7N4KJu6";
$url = "http://worldcat.org/webservices/catalog/search/worldcat/";
$url .= "opensearch?q=".$query;
$url .= "&start=".$start;
$url .= "&count=".$count;
$url .= "&cformat=".$cformat;
$url .= "&wskey=".$key;
```

Now, remember that we are still in the `for` loop. For each ISBN we are constructing a URL request for WorldCat Basic data.

Next comes a critically important step that involves using cURL. The process is fully explicated in the WorldCat Basic API in Action section. Read that section first to fully understand the process here.

```
$ch = curl_init($url);
curl_setopt($ch, CURLOPT_RETURNTRANSFER, true);
curl_setopt($ch, CURLOPT_HEADER, 0);
$data = curl_exec($ch);
curl_close($ch);
$doc = new SimpleXmlElement($data, LIBXML_NOCDATA);
$count = count($doc->entry);
```

To finish the script we will introduce another `for` loop. Note that there will be a `for` loop within a `for` loop. This requires us to name the variables differently. Thus:

```
for ($j = 0; $j < $count; $j++) {
```

Typically in a `for` loop, the variable is set as `$i`. Since we have a nested `for` loop, we've changed it to `$j`.

Now to finish the script. Remember to close out both `for` loops, print out a closing `</ul>` tag, and end the PHP script.

```
print '<li><a href=' . $doc->entry[$j]->id . '>' . $doc->entry[$j]->title .
    '</a> by ' . $doc->entry[$j]->author->name . '<br />' .
    $doc->entry[$j]->content . '</li>';
}
}
print '</ul>';
?>
```

So for each ISBN, the WorldCat Basic API is returning a title (hyperlinked back to the WorldCat record), the author, and an MLA citation.

- A game of thrones by Martin, George R. R.
  Martin, George R. R. *A Game of Thrones*. New York: Bantam Books, 1996. Print.
- A game of thrones : Book one of A song of ice and fire by Martin, George R. R.
  Martin, George R. R. *A Game of Thrones: Book One of a Song of Ice and Fire*. New York: Bantam Books, 1996. Print.
- A game of thrones / Book 1 by Martin, George R. R.
  Martin, George R. R. *A Game of Thrones: Book 1*. New York: Bantam Books, 1996. Print.
- A game of thrones by Martin, George R. R.
  Martin, George R. R. *A Game of Thrones: Bk. 1*. New York: Bantam Books, 1996. Print.
- A Game of Thrones by Martin, George R. R.
  Martin, George R. R. *A Game of Thrones*. 1540 Broadway, New York, New York 10036: Bantam Books, 1996. Print.
- A game of thrones by Martin, George R. R.
  Martin, George R. R. *A Game of Thrones*. New York: Bantam Books, 1997. Internet resource.
- A game of thrones by Martin, George R. R.
  Martin, George R. R., and Roy Dotrice. *A Game of Thrones*. Santa Ana, Calif.: Books on Tape, 2004. Internet resource.
- Game of thrones by Martin, George R. R.
  Martin, George R. R., and Roy Dotrice. *Game of Thrones*. Santa Ana, CA: Books on Tape, 2004. Sound recording.
- A game of thrones by Martin, George R. R.
  Martin, George R. R. *A Game of Thrones*. New York: Bantam Books, 1997. Print.

Here's the complete script:

```
<?php
$xisbn = "0553103547";
$xmethod = "getEditions";
$xformat = "json";
$xurl = "http://xisbn.worldcat.org/webservices/xid/isbn/$xisbn";
$xurl .= "?method=$xmethod";
$xurl .= "&format=$xformat";
$xraw_data = file_get_contents($xurl);
$xdata = json_decode($xraw_data);
$xcount = count($xdata->list);
echo $xcount;
print '<!DOCTYPE HTML PUBLIC "-//W3C//DTD HTML 4.01 Transitional//EN" "http://
    www.w3.org/TR/html4/loose.dtd">';
print '<html>';
print '<head>
```

```
        <meta http-equiv="Content-Type" content="text/html; charset=utf-8">
        </head>';
print '<ul>';
for ($i = 0; $i < $xcount; $i++) {
    $query = $xdata->list[$i]->isbn[0];
    $format = "atom";
    $start = "1";
    $count = "10";
    $cformat = "mla";
    $key = "your_key_here";
    $url = "http://worldcat.org/webservices/catalog/search/worldcat/";
    $url .= "opensearch?q=".$query;
    $url .= "&format=".$format;
    $url .= "&start=".$start;
    $url .= "&count=".$count;
    $url .= "&cformat=".$cformat;
    $url .= "&wskey=".$key;
    $ch = curl_init($url);
    curl_setopt ($ch, CURLOPT_RETURNTRANSFER, true);
    curl_setopt($ch, CURLOPT_HEADER, 0);
    $data = curl_exec($ch);
    curl_close($ch);
    $doc = new SimpleXmlElement($data, LIBXML_NOCDATA);
    $count = count($doc->entry);
    for ($j = 0; $j < $count; $j++) {
        print '<li><a href=' . $doc->entry[$j]->id . '>' . $doc->entry[$j]->title
        . '</a> by ' . $doc->entry[$j]->author->name . '<br />' . $doc
        ->entry[$j]->content . '</li>';
    }
}
print '</ul>';
?>
```

WORLDCAT XISSN API

The WorldCat xISSN API provides serials data programmatically. Supplied with an ISSN, the API returns valuable data such as preceding and succeeding ISSNs, serial titles, serial formats, and coverage dates. In order to utilize the API, you must obtain an affiliate account from OCLC. Go to www.worldcat.org/wcpa/content/affiliate/ to register.

As with WorldCat's xISBN API, the xISSN service works via a URL request. The base URL string is

```
http://xissn.worldcat.org/webservices/xid/issn/
```

There are several parameters for this request:

PARAMETER	MEANING	REQUIRED
issn	ISSN value	Yes
method	Determines the data the xISSN service will return; options include getForms, getEditions, getHistory, and getMetadata	Yes
format	Format of data returned; supported formats are XML, JSON, CSV, TEXT, Python, Ruby, XHTML	Yes
ai	Affiliate ID	Yes

As you can see, the xISSN service has several methods to choose from. For a full-featured list of these methods, go to http://xissn.worldcat.org/xissnadmin/doc/api.htm#getforms.

WORLDCAT XISSN API IN ACTION

This script will illustrate how you can utilize the API to return associated titles, their respective ISSNs and formats, their coverage dates, and links to their RSS feeds if available.

Let's begin the script by declaring a variable and supplying it with an initial ISSN value:

```php
<?php
$issn = "1541-1672";
```

Remember that in a live situation, this ISSN would get pulled in from your catalog data. To get an idea of the type of data returned for each method, we will create an array of methods upon which we will perform actions. Throughout this book, you have worked with arrays by parsing already existing arrays. For this example we will also create an array. Just follow along with the example and it will work out for you. The next line should be

```
$method = array("getForms", "getEditions", "getHistory", "getMetadata");
```

Here we are creating an array, `$method`, of all the available methods for the xISSN service. Now that we have done that, let's declare the rest of our variables:

```
$format = "json";
$ai = "your_affiliate_id";
```

Next we will set up a `for` loop that will utilize each method and print out the data for each in a respective array. This is helpful for visualizing the data that you have to work with:

```
$count = count($method);
for ($i = 0; $i < $count; $i++) {
print '<h2>' . $method[$i] . '</h2>';
```

The above line will print out the name of the method above its array, making it easier to see what array belongs to which method. We will continue the script by declaring the base URL in a variable:

```
$url = "http://xissn.worldcat.org/webservices/xid/issn/";
```

Now that we have the base URL in a variable, we can concatenate the base string with our parameters:

```
$url .= "$issn";
```

The next parameter that we need to append to the URL is the method. Because we are working with an array of methods, we will need to concatenate this way:

```
$url .= "?method=$method[$i]";
```

Remember that we are in a `for` loop, so the first time that the script goes through the loop, it will read the above line as `$url .= "?method=$method[0]";` and therefore create a request URL that utilizes the `getForms` method (get Forms being the 0 index in our custom array).

Let's finish up the URL variables:

```
$url .= "&format=$format";
$url .= "&ai=$ai";
```

Our URL is now constructed, so let's use that variable to go out and grab the data:

```
$raw_data = file_get_contents($url);
```

The returned data is in JSON format, so we will need to use the `json_decode` function to place it in a well-formed PHP array variable:

```
$data = json_decode($raw_data);
```

Now print the data out and close the `for` loop:

```
print '<pre>';
print_r ($data);
print '</pre>';
}
```

Save your file and open it up via a browser. You should see four PHP objects with embedded arrays of data, each preceded by a heading denoting the name of the method. It should look like this:

```
getForms
stdClass Object
(
 [stat] => ok
 [group] => Array
    (
       [0] => stdClass Object
        (
          [rel] => this
          [list] => Array
             (
                [0] => stdClass Object
                 (
                    [issn] => 1941-1294
                    [form] => JD
                 )
                [1] => stdClass Object
                 (
                    [issn] => 1094-7167
                    [form] => JB
                 )
                [2] => stdClass Object
                 (
                    [issn] => 1541-1672
                    [form] => JD
                 )
```

```
                    [3] => stdClass Object
                      (
                          [issn] => 0885-9000
                          [form] => JB
                      )  .
                )
            )
        )
    )
getEditions
stdClass Object
(
 [stat] => ok
 [group] => Array
    (
        [0] => stdClass Object
         (
           [rel] => this
           [list] => Array
              (
                  [0] => stdClass Object
                    (
                        [rssurl] => http://ieeexplore.ieee.org/rss/TOC9670.XML
                        [publisher] => Los Alamitos, CA : IEEE Computer Society
                        [form] => JD
                        [peerreview] => Y
                        [rawcoverage] => Vol. 16, no. 1 (Jan./Feb. 2001)-
                        [title] => IEEE intelligent systems
                        [issn] => 1941-1294
                        [oclcnum] => Array
                           (
                               [0] => 44579208
                           )
                        [issnl] => 1541-1672
                    ) . . . etc.
```

Go back to the code and let's continue. What we are going to do first is print out the ISSNs and their respective formats:

```
print '<h2>Formats</h2>';
```

We already have many of the variables declared earlier in the script. We will just need to construct the URL again, this time using the `getForms` method:

```
$url = "http://xissn.worldcat.org/webservices/xid/issn/";
$url .= "$issn";
$url .= "?method=$method[0]";
$url .= "&format=$format";
$url .= "&ai=$ai";
$raw_data = file_get_contents($url);
$data = json_decode($raw_data);
```

Now we have the returned PHP object that `getForms` gives us. The data that is interesting to us is in the `list` array, so we will make that array its own variable:

```
$forms = $data->group[0]->list;
```

To get an idea of what this array looks like, use `print_r` on the variable:

```
print '<pre>';
print_r ($forms);
print '</pre>';
```

The array should look like this when you view it in the browser:

```
Array
(
[0] => stdClass Object
    (
        [issn] => 1941-1294
        [form] => JD
    )
[1] => stdClass Object
    (
        [issn] => 1094-7167
        [form] => JB
    )
[2] => stdClass Object
    (
        [issn] => 1541-1672
        [form] => JD
    )
[3] => stdClass Object
    (
        [issn] => 0885-9000
        [form] => JB
    )
)
```

As you can see, there are two data fields: `form` and `issn`. The `form` field is occupied with a code. The potential codes in this field are: JB (printed serial), JC (serial distributed electronically by carrier), JD (electronic serial distributed online), and MA (microform). We can use this knowledge to print out the format.

To continue, we will build a `for` loop to go through each section of the array and print out the format and its respective ISSN:

```
$forms_count = count($forms);
echo $forms_count;
for ($j = 0; $j < $forms_count; $j++) {
if ($forms[$j]->form == "JD") {
```

Here we are using `if` logic to determine what we will be printing out to the screen. So, for example, if JD is in the form field, then we know that it is an electronic serial. If this is the case, we will print "Digital" to the screen followed by its ISSN. If the form is JB then we will print "Print" to the screen, and so forth:

```
    print '<p>Digital:' . $forms[$j]->issn . '</p>';
}
elseif ($forms[$j]->form == "JB") {
    print '<p>Print:' . $forms[$j]->issn . '</p>';
}
elseif ($forms[$j]->form == "JC") {
    print '<p>Digital distributed by carrier:' . $forms[$j]->issn . '</p>';
}
elseif ($forms[$j]->form == "MA") {
    print '<p>Microform:' . $forms[$j]->issn . '</p>';
}
}
```

Save this file and view it in a browser. You should see something simple like the box at right:

Let's move on to the `getEditions` method. This method returns a bit more data to work with. Using this method we will print out the title associated with each ISSN and its respective format and ISSN and include a hyperlink to the serial's RSS feed if available:

```
print '<h2>Editions</h2>';
$url = "http://xissn.worldcat.org/webservices/xid/issn/";
$url .= "$issn";
$url .= "?method=$method[1]";
$url .= "&format=$format";
$url .= "&ai=$ai";
$raw_data = file_get_contents($url);
$data = json_decode($raw_data);
```

Formats

4

Digital:1941-1294

Print:1094-7167

Digital:1541-1672

Print:0885-9000

Now we have the returned PHP object that `getEditions` gives us. The data that is interesting to us is in the `list` array, so we will make that array its own variable:

```
$eds = $data->group[0]->list;
```

To visualize what this array looks like, use `print_r` on the variable:

```
print '<pre>';
print_r ($eds);
print '</pre>';
```

Compared to the `getForms` method, we have more data to work with: RSS URL, publisher, form, peer review, raw coverage, title, ISSN, and related OCLC number. With this script we will pull out the RSS URL, form, title, ISSN, and raw coverage, though it would be interesting to utilize the `peerreview` field. Try that on your own.

Let's continue by building a `for` loop to go through the array. As before, we will apply `if` logic to print out the correct format:

```
$eds_count = count($eds);
echo $eds_count;
for ($h = 0; $h < $eds_count; $h++) {
if ($eds[$h]->form == "JD") {
   print '<h3><a href="' . $eds[$h]->rssurl . '">' . $eds[$h]->title. '</a>
      </h2>';
   print '<p>Digital:' . $eds[$h]->issn . ' Coverage: ' . $eds[$h]->rawcoverage
      . '</p>';
}
elseif ($eds[$h]->form == "JB") {
   print '<h3><a href="' . $eds[$h]->rssurl . '">' . $eds[$h]->title. '</a>
      </h2>';
   print '<p>Print:' . $eds[$h]->issn . ' Coverage: ' . $eds[$h]->rawcoverage
      . '</p>';
}
elseif ($eds[$h]->form == "JC") {
   print '<h3><a href="' . $eds[$h]->rssurl . '">' . $eds[$h]->title. '</a>
      </h2>';
   print '<p>Digital distributed by carrier:' . $eds[$h]->issn . ' Coverage: '
      . $eds[$h]->rawcoverage . '</p>';
}
elseif ($eds[$h]->form == "MA") {
   print '<h3><a href="' . $eds[$h]->rssurl . '">' . $eds[$h]->title. '</a>
      </h2>';
```

```
    print '<p>Microform:' . $eds[$h]->issn . ' Coverage: ' . $eds[$h]->
       rawcoverage . '</p>';
  }
}
?>
```

Close off the `for` loop and end with a closing PHP tag as shown. Save your file and open it up via the browser. You should see something similar to this:

Editions

4

IEEE intelligent systems

Digital:1941-1294 Coverage: Vol. 16, no. 1 (Jan./Feb. 2001)-

IEEE intelligent systems & their applications

Print:1094-7167 Coverage: Vol. 12, no. 6 (Nov./Dec. 1997)-v. 15, no. 6 (Nov./Dec. 2000).

IEEE intelligent systems

Digital:1541-1672 Coverage: Vol. 16, no. 1 (Jan./Feb. 2001)-

IEEE expert

Print:0885-9000 Coverage: Vol. 1, no. 1 (spring 1986)-v. 12, no. 5 (Sept./Oct. 1997).

Experiment with this script by substituting new ISSNs. You can see how an application like this could be implemented into a library serials service.

Here's the complete, unadulterated script:

```php
<?php
$issn = "0972-0073";
$method = array("getForms", "getEditions", "getHistory", "getMetadata");
$format = "json";
$ai = "enter affiliate id";
$count = count($method);
for ($i = 0; $i < $count; $i++) {
print '<h2>' . $method[$i] . '</h2>';
$url = "http://xissn.worldcat.org/webservices/xid/issn/";
$url .= "$issn";
$url .= "?method=$method[$i]";
$url .= "&format=$format";
$url .= "&ai=$ai";
$raw_data = file_get_contents($url);
$data = json_decode($raw_data);
```

```
print '<pre>';
print_r ($data);
print '</pre>';
}
print '<h2>Formats</h2>';
$url = "http://xissn.worldcat.org/webservices/xid/issn/";
$url .= "$issn";
$url .= "?method=$method[0]";
$url .= "&format=$format";
$url .= "&ai=$ai";
$raw_data = file_get_contents($url);
$data = json_decode($raw_data);
$forms = $data->group[0]->list;
$forms_count = count($forms);
echo $forms_count;
for ($j = 0; $j < $forms_count; $j++) {
if ($forms[$j]->form == "JD") {
   print '<p>Digital:' . $forms[$j]->issn . '</p>';
}
elseif ($forms[$j]->form == "JB") {
   print '<p>Print:' . $forms[$j]->issn . '</p>';
}
elseif ($forms[$j]->form == "JC") {
   print '<p>Digital distributed by carrier:' . $forms[$j]->issn . '</p>';
}
elseif ($forms[$j]->form == "MA") {
   print '<p>Microform:' . $forms[$j]->issn . '</p>';
}
}
print '<h2>Editions</h2>';
$url = "http://xissn.worldcat.org/webservices/xid/issn/";
$url .= "$issn";
$url .= "?method=$method[1]";
$url .= "&format=$format";
$url .= "&ai=$ai";
$raw_data = file_get_contents($url);
$data = json_decode($raw_data);
$eds = $data->group[0]->list;
$eds_count = count($eds);
echo $eds_count;
for ($h = 0; $h < $eds_count; $h++) {
if ($eds[$h]->form == "JD") {
   print '<h3><a href="' . $eds[$h]->rssurl . '">' . $eds[$h]->title. '</a>
      </h2>';
   print '<p>Digital:' . $eds[$h]->issn . ' Coverage: ' . $eds[$h]->rawcoverage
      . '</p>';
```

```
}
elseif ($eds[$h]->form == "JB") {
    print '<h3><a href="' . $eds[$h]->rssurl . '">' . $eds[$h]->title. '</a>
        </h2>';
    print '<p>Print:' . $eds[$h]->issn . ' Coverage: ' . $eds[$h]->rawcoverage .
        '</p>';
}
elseif ($eds[$h]->form == "JC") {
    print '<h3><a href="' . $eds[$h]->rssurl . '">' . $eds[$h]->title. '</a>
        </h2>';
    print '<p>Digital distributed by carrier:' . $eds[$h]->issn . ' Coverage: '
        . $eds[$h]->rawcoverage . '</p>';
}
elseif ($eds[$h]->form == "MA") {
    print '<h3><a href="' . $eds[$h]->rssurl . '">' . $eds[$h]->title. '</a>
        </h2>';
    print '<p>Microform:' . $eds[$h]->issn . ' Coverage: ' .
        $eds[$h]->rawcoverage . '</p>';
}
}
?>
```

CHAPTER SIX

HATHITRUST API AND LIBRARIES

HathiTrust is an open digital preservation repository that provides access to millions of public domain and in-copyright e-books and other content. This content comes from many sources, including Google, the Internet Archive, Microsoft, and participating institutions such as the University of Michigan, the New York Public Library, and more.

The content that Hathi provides, especially the public domain content, can bring added value and additional content to your collections and provide your users with easy access to the full text of millions of public domain works.

HathiTrust is dedicated to maintaining an open infrastructure and providing the best means possible for data retrieval and manipulation; thus its various APIs are quite robust and at the same time simple to use.

HathiTrust has two primary APIs: Bib API and Data API. We will be discussing and implementing scripts based on the Bib API.

HATHITRUST BIB API TECHNICAL DETAILS

The HathiTrust Bib API returns bibliographic data when given an ID number such as an ISBN or OCLC Control Number.

The base request URL is

```
http://catalog.hathitrust.org/api/volumes/
```

Appended to this base URL is the record type you are interested in obtaining. Hathi returns either a `full` or `brief` record. The `full` record returns the complete MARC-XML for the item in question. Finally, you'll append the ID type followed by the actual ID and data file type. Currently, HathiTrust uses only JSON. Thus:

```
http://catalog.hathitrust.org/api/volumes/full/oclc/381593.json
```

The Bib API does not require an API key or any other authentication. To see the raw data that is returned simply type the above URL into your browser and examine the results.

What is returned is the raw JSON data structure.

PARAMETER	MEANING	REQUIRED
`type`	ID type to search on; accepted IDs are `oclc`, `lccn`, `isbn`, `issn`, `htid` (HathiTrust ID), and `recordnumber`	Yes
`id`	ID number	Yes
`level`	Type and amount of data returned; `brief` or `full` (`full` returns full MARC-XML)	Yes

HATHITRUST BIB API IN ACTION

Since the HathiTrust Bib API works when given a known ID, we will supply the script with a value. In a live application, you could pull this value from records returned on a search query.

Begin the script by declaring your variables:

```php
<?php
$type = "oclc";
$id = "381593";
$level = "full";
```

Here you can switch out `oclc` for any of the other accepted ID types. The `$id` variable is the actual ID number associated with the `$type` variable. `$level` indicates whether you want full or brief records. The full record will return the complete MARC-XML for the item. Now that we have our parameter variables set, we can declare our request URL variable:

```
$url = "http://catalog.hathitrust.org/api/volumes/";
```

This is the base URL onto which we need to concatenate our parameter variables:

```
$url .= "$level";
$url .= "/$type";
$url .= "/$id.";
$url .= "json";
```

Before continuing with the script, let's `echo` out the URL to ensure that it is formatted properly:

```
echo $url;
```

If you see this in the browser window then your URL is properly constructed:

http://catalog.hathitrust.org/api/volumes/full/oclc/381593.json

Let's continue with the script:

```
$raw_data = file_get_contents($url);
$data = json_decode($raw_data);
```

We have done these two PHP functions before. Again, what it is doing is grabbing the data and putting it into a variable called `$raw_data`, then it is decoding that data from JSON and storing it in a PHP object called `$data`. Now that it is stored in a PHP object, we can interact with and manipulate that data.

To get a sense of the type of data returned and its structure, type the following lines into the script:

```
print '<pre>';
print_r ($data);
print '</pre>';
```

You should see a typical PHP object once you open your browser:

```
stdClass Object
(
 [records] => stdClass Object
    (
```

```
        [001505930] => stdClass Object
          (
            [recordURL] => http://catalog.hathitrust.org/Record/001505930
            [titles] => Array
              (
                 [0] => Making a garden of perennials,
              )
            . . .
            [oclcs] => Array
              (
                 [0] => 381593
              )
            [lccns] => Array
              (
                 [0] => 12016606
              )
            [publishDates] => Array
              (
                 [0] => 1912
              )
            [marc-xml] => 00000nam a22002291  4500001505930MiU19890828000000.
    0m          d          cr bn ---auaua890828s1912    nyu              00000 eng
    d12016606sdr-nrlfGLAD33760118-B(CaOTULAS)176496784(SAZTEC)128102700(OCo
    LC)ocm00381593sdr-nyp.b135640738sdr-ia-nrlf.b129679380CarPSB453.E4Egan,
    W. C.(William Constantine),1841-1930.Making a garden of perennials,New
    York,McBride, Nast & company,1912.5 p.l., 52 p.8 pl. (incl. front.)17
    cm.Mode of access: Internet.GardeningFloricultureMiUBUHRGRADSB 405
    .E28uc1SDRNRLFnypSDRNYPuc2SDRINRLFBKBookMiU20040625HTavail_htHAavail_
    ht_fulltextAOavail_onlineACavail_circmdp.39015063987559pd20090719
    nyp.33433006561918pd20100924uc1.b278496pd20090930uc2.ark:/13960/
    t8w952701pd20110208UTL9662
          )
      )
[items] => Array
    (
        [0] => stdClass Object
          (
            [orig] => University of California
            [fromRecord] => 001505930
            [htid] => uc2.ark:/13960/t8w952701
            [itemURL] => http://hdl.handle.net/2027/uc2.ark:/13960/t8w952701
            [rightsCode] => pd
            [lastUpdate] => 20110208
            [enumcron] =>
            [usRightsString] => Full view
          )
```

```
       . . .
      [3] => stdClass Object
       (
          [orig] => University of Michigan
          [fromRecord] => 001505930
          [htid] => mdp.39015063987559
          [itemURL] => http://hdl.handle.net/2027/mdp.39015063987559
          [rightsCode] => pd
          [lastUpdate] => 20090719
          [enumcron] =>
          [usRightsString] => Full view
       )
    )
 )
```

The object that is returned has two primary sections. The first, `[records]`, contains bibliographic data such as the title, ID numbers, and the complete MARC-XML. The second, `[items]`, includes data on the actual items hosted in the repository, such as institution, rights information, and URL to the actual item.

Now that we have the data in a proper PHP object, we can pull it out and display it via HTML. The first thing that we will print to the screen will be the title of the book. This will require a little bit of extra coding since the title is included in array which is in an object indexed by the HathiTrust ID. Now, we don't know the HathiTrust ID, so we cannot hand-code it in there to pull up the title. Thankfully, the Hathi ID is listed for each record in the `[items]` array in the field `[from Record]`.

To make the Hathi ID more portable and easier to use in the script, let's first put it into a variable.

Look at the printed data in this section:

```
 . . .
[items] => Array
 (
    [0] => stdClass Object
      (
        [orig] => University of California
        [fromRecord] => 001505930
        [htid] => uc2.ark:/13960/t8w952701
        [itemURL] => http://hdl.handle.net/2027/uc2.ark:/13960/t8w952701
        [rightsCode] => pd
        [lastUpdate] => 20110208
        [enumcron] =>
        [usRightsString] => Full view
      )
 . . .
```

The `[fromRecord]` field contains the Hathi ID. To place that number into a variable we will use this one line of code:

```
$record = $data->items[0]->fromRecord;
```

To test this variable use the `echo` command:

```
echo $record;
```

When you reopen this file in the browser, you should see 001505930 printed out to the screen. Now that it is in a variable, we can more easily use it in other parts of the script.

Before continuing, comment out this line (or delete it entirely):

```
//echo $record;
```

Again, the primary reason we need to get the Hathi ID (now stored in the `$record` variable) is to be able to grab the title of the book, which is stored here:

```
stdClass Object
(
[records] => stdClass Object
    (
        [001505930] => stdClass Object
        (
            [recordURL] => http://catalog.hathitrust.org/Record/001505930
            [titles] => Array
                (
                    [0] => Making a garden of perennials,
                )
. . .
```

Without knowing the Hathi ID, we wouldn't be able to get into that object. Now that we have the ID, we can get at the title with this line, where we are placing the title in a portable variable:

```
$title = $data->records->$record->titles[0];
```

Now that we have the necessary data in variables, we can simple print out the title as a heading in HTML:

```
print '<h2>' . $title . '</h2>';
```

In addition to the title, let's print out a hyperlink to the actual book display in Hathi, so users can read it:

```php
print '<a href="' . $data->items[0]->itemURL . '">Read Online at HathiTrust
    </a>';
```

This bit of code could be modified to fit in to your catalog and would give your users an additional e-book option, if, for example the book is checked out.

---

http://catalog.hathitrust.org/api/volumes/full/oclc/381593.json

Making a garden of perennials,

Read Online at HathiTrust

Here's the full script:

```php
<?php
$type = "oclc";
$id = "381593";
$level = "full";
$url = "http://catalog.hathitrust.org/api/volumes/";
$url .= "$level";
$url .= "/$type";
$url .= "/$id.";
$url .= "json";
echo $url;
$raw_data = file_get_contents($url);
$data = json_decode($raw_data);
$record = $data->items[0]->fromRecord;
$title = $data->records->$record->titles[0];
print '<h2>' . $title . '</h2>';
print '<a href="' . $data->items[0]->itemURL . '">Read online at HathiTrust
    </a>';
?>
```

CHAPTER SEVEN

OPEN LIBRARY API AND LIBRARIES

Open Library (openlibrary.org) is a web service dedicated to creating "one web page for every book ever published." It is essentially a crowdsourced catalog of bibliographic information with open data and open APIs. Anyone can add an entry or edit a page. It is a collaborative project with the Internet Archive. To date, Open Library has over 20 million records.

A typical record in the Open Library displays a book cover if available, standard publication information, edition notes, genre, LC and Dewey classifications, a physical description, and ID numbers, including ID numbers for LibraryThing and Goodreads.

In addition, most records include embedded MARC records (where much of the data is initially generated).

Besides including bibliographic data, Open Library records link out to commercial vendors such as Amazon.com and AbeBooks; link out to WorldCat for library holdings; and if there is an e-book available, provide an interface to either read or download the e-book.

Like most crowdsourced wikis, Open Library maintains a revision history; allowing users to see the changes that have been made over the life of a record.

Open Library offers several APIs to developers. This section of the book will cover two primary APIs: Books API and Covers API.

OPEN LIBRARY BOOKS API TECHNICAL DETAILS

Like the Twitter Search API and other APIs discussed in this book, the Open Library Books API is based on URL requests. No key or other authentication is necessary to interact with the data.

The Books API returns an abundance of bibliographic data that can be integrated into your applications.

To get started, let's take a look at the base URL request format:

```
http://openlibrary.org/api/books?
```

This is the base URL upon which we will add our parameters to effectively query the API.

PARAMETER	MEANING	REQUIRED
`bibkeys`	ID used to search Open Library; accepts ISBN, LCCN, OCLC numbers, OLIDs (Open Library IDs)	Yes
`format`	Format of data returned; either JSON or JavaScript	No; if left out, it will default to JavaScript
`callback`	Specifies name of JavaScript function to call with result	No; include `callback` only if JavaScript is being used as format
`jscmd`	Determines type of information provided; `viewapi` returns cover and hyperlinks; `data` returns all bibliographic data.	No; if left out, it will default to `viewapi`

Considering these parameters, let's add them to the base URL request format and point our browsers to that URL:

http://openlibrary.org/api/books?bibkeys=OCLC:4942988&jscmd=data&
format=json

What you will see is a slew of data in JSON format about on particular title, the Coburn Players acting edition of *The Tragedy of Macbeth*.

Let's see the API in action in a basic application that displays the cover of the title, basic publication information, download links, and links back to Open Library. Since we want to include bibliographic information and cover images and links back to the original Open Library record, we will need to construct two distinct URL requests: one that sets `jscmd` to `viewapi` and one that sets it to `data`.

OPEN LIBRARY BOOKS API IN ACTION

As with the other APIs in this book, this script will be written in PHP. Create a new .php file in your favorite text editor. To get started let's declare our parameter variables:

```php
<?php
$bibkeys = "OCLC:4942988";
$format = "json";
$jscmd = "data";
```

For this example, please use the book that I'm referencing with the OCLC number. Certainly, you can experiment with others, but I know that this OCLC will return e-book resources, which I want to illustrate for you.

Notice that the `$jscmd` at this point is `data`. This will return all of the bibliographic data. We need to get this data separately from our cover image and links back to Open Library. Again, we will construct two separate request URLs.

Now let's begin to construct our URL. We will do this in the same way we constructed our WorldCat Basic API request URL—that is, iteratively:

```php
$url = "http://openlibrary.org/api/books?";
$url .= "bibkeys=$bibkeys";
$url .= "&jscmd=$jscmd";
$url .= "&format=$format";
```

Now we have all of the parameters appended to the base URL and are ready to pull in the data based on that URL request:

```php
$raw_data = file_get_contents($url);
```

What this function is doing is populating `$raw_data` with the returned JSON data as a string. To take a peek at what this looks like add the following lines, upload your PHP file to your web server, and point your browser to the file:

```php
print '<pre>';
echo $raw_data;
print '</pre>';
```

What you'll see is a long string of JSON data. To continue the script add this line:

```
$data = json_decode($raw_data);
```

This function takes the JSON-encoded data within `$raw_data` and converts it to a PHP variable—in other words, `$data` that we can manipulate.

Examine the differences between `$data` and `$raw_data` by printing out `$data`:

```
print '<pre>';
print_r ($data);
print '</pre>';
```

Printing out `$data` in this fashion allows you to visualize all of the data you have at your disposal. As we continue writing this script, it will be helpful for you to continue to print out `$data`, as this will allow you to see all of the variables and how they can be extracted from either an array or an object they may be embedded within.

Let's begin printing out the HTML markup:

```
print '<!DOCTYPE HTML PUBLIC "-//W3C//DTD HTML 4.01 Transitional//EN" "http://
    www.w3.org/TR/html4/loose.dtd">';
print '<html>';
print '<head>
   <meta http-equiv="Content-Type" content="text/html; charset=utf-8">
   <title>Open Library Books API | Demo</title>
   </head>';
```

For this basic example, we will print out the book cover and place appropriate information next to it. Let's start with the book cover. To do that, we first need to find it in the `$data` variable. Again, go to your browser and take a look at the printed out `$data` variable.

For simplicity's sake, I'll print it out here:

```
stdClass Object
(
[OCLC:4942988] => stdClass Object
    (
        [publishers] => Array
         (
           [0] => stdClass Object
             (
                 [name] => The Coburn players
             )
         )
```

```
    [cover] => stdClass Object
(
    [small] => http://covers.openlibrary.org/b/id/6849239-S.jpg
    [large] => http://covers.openlibrary.org/b/id/6849239-L.jpg
    [medium] => http://covers.openlibrary.org/b/id/6849239-M.jpg
)
```

I've deleted several lines to keep things simple. If you look in the variable here, you'll see that `cover` is an object with three available resources: `small`, `large`, and `medium`.

To print out the cover, type the following line into the script:

```
print '<img src="' . $data->$bibkeys->cover->medium . '" />';
```

This is how you extract data out of PHP objects. First you identify the variable, in this case `$data`. Then you identify the distinct object within that variable, which in our case is `[OCLC:4942988]`. You can see this in the third line of the printed `$data` variable. Once you are in the `$bibkeys` object you can drill down to `cover` and finally `medium`. If you wanted a large cover you would replace `medium` with `large`.

Now we can print out the title and author of the work:

```
print '<h2>' . $data->$bibkeys->title . '</h2>';
print '<p>by ' . $data->$bibkeys->authors[0]->name . '</p>';
```

The Open Library API is very rich with data, and because of that we can enhance what we've got further by hyperlinking both the title and the author. That way, users can easily jump to the Open Library work page or author page.

```
print '<h2><a href="' . $data->$bibkeys->url . '">' . $data->$bibkeys->title
    . '</a></h2>';
print '<p>by <a href="' . $data->$bibkeys->authors[0]->url . '">' . $data
    ->$bibkeys->authors[0]->name . '</a></p>';
```

All we did here was create hyperlinks to the URLs that are embedded within the `$data` object; specifically, the URLs found within `$data->$bibkeys ->url` (which links to the main page of the work) and `$data->$bibkeys ->authors[0]->url` (which links to the author page).

Let's now display some of the subjects that are listed in the bibliographic record. This will be a useful exercise since the subjects are an array of objects within `$data` and thus require a `for` loop to get more than one of them.

```
print '<p>Subjects:</p>';
print '<ul>';
$subject_count = count($data->$bibkeys->subjects);
```

Okay, so the line above is determining how many subjects are listed as an array in the `subjects` object. This count, stored in `$subject_count`, will be used in the following `for` loop logic:

```
for ($i = 0; $i < $subject_count; $i++) {
```

This is the standard syntax for `for` loops. What it is saying is first `$i` equals 0; then it is saying that while `$i` is less than `$subject_count` do whatever is held within the `for` loop (printing out the subjects). Finally, the code is incrementally adding to `$i` each time it runs through the loop, so that by the time `$i` is no longer less than `$subject_count` it will have run through all of the subjects in the array.

The next line is

```
print '<li>' . $data->$bibkeys->subjects[$i]->name . '</li>';
```

This is what is being printed out every cycle of the `for` loop. End the `for` loop and print out a closing to the unordered HTML list:

```
}
print '</ul>';
```

Point your browser to the URL and take a look. There should be a long list of subjects.

We can edit this list a bit, since there are dozens of subjects listed and the most important and relevant subjects are near the top. If you are interested in printing out only the top five subjects, you can edit the first line of the `for` loop:

```
for ($i = 0; $i < 5; $i++) {
```

Now the `for` loop will cycle through only five times.

As we did previously with the title and the author, we can hyperlink these subjects to Open Library's subject pages. To do this, simply replace the `print` command in the `for` loop with this one:

```
print '<li><a href="' . $data->$bibkeys->subjects[$i]->url . '">' . $data
    ->$bibkeys->subjects[$i]->name . '</a></li>';
```

As you can see, it still prints out the subjects; but now it hyperlinks them as well.

To integrate this even more fully into your resources, you could take these subjects and create hyperlinks to subject searches in your catalog. For example,

```
print '<li><a href="http://www.lib.muohio.edu/multifacet/books/' . $data
    ->$bibkeys->subjects[$i]->name . '?field=subjects">' . $data->$bibkeys
    ->subjects[$i]->name . '</a></li>';
```

If you paste this into your code, it will print out a list of the subjects linking to the Miami University Libraries' catalog. Try it with your catalog!

Finally, let's provide download links for the various e-book formats available:

```
print '<p>Download:</p>';
print '<ul>';
print '<li><a href="' . $data->$bibkeys->ebooks[0]->formats->pdf->url .
    '">Download the PDF</a></li>';
print '<li><a href="' . $data->$bibkeys->ebooks[0]->formats->epub->url .
    '">Download the ePub</a></li>';
print '</ul>';
```

You could also link directly to Open Library's interface to read the item. Open Library's Reading functionality is very impressive. It includes a variety of viewing options and in some cases contains an option that reads the text aloud:

```
print '<p><a href="' . $data->$bibkeys->ebooks[0]->read_url . '">Read Now!</a>';
```

The potentiality of adding easily accessible e-book formats to your existing catalog is particularly appealing. Opening doors to your users as opposed to leading them to dead ends will increase the likelihood that they will continue to use your catalog and other resources.

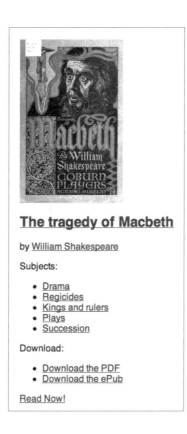

Here's the complete script:

```php
<?php
$bibkeys = "OCLC:4942988";
$format = "json";
$jscmd = "data";
$url = "http://openlibrary.org/api/books?";
$url .= "bibkeys=$bibkeys";
$url .= "&jscmd=$jscmd";
$url .= "&format=$format";
$raw_data = file_get_contents($url);
$data = json_decode($raw_data);
print '<!DOCTYPE HTML PUBLIC "-//W3C//DTD HTML 4.01 Transitional//EN" "http://
    www.w3.org/TR/html4/loose.dtd">';
print '<html>';
print '<head>
    <meta http-equiv="Content-Type" content="text/html; charset=utf-8">
    <title>Open Library Books API | Demo</title>
    </head>';
print '<img src="' . $data->$bibkeys->cover->medium . '" />';
print '<h2><a href="' . $data->$bibkeys->url . '">' . $data->$bibkeys->title
    . '</a></h2>';
print '<p>by <a href="' . $data->$bibkeys->authors[0]->url . '">' . $data
    ->$bibkeys->authors[0]->name . '</a></p>';
print '<p>Subjects:</p>';
print '<ul>';
$subject_count = count($data->$bibkeys->subjects);
for ($i = 0; $i < 5; $i++) {
print '<li><a href="' . $data->$bibkeys->subjects[$i]->url . '">' . $data
    ->$bibkeys->subjects[$i]->name . '</a></li>';
print '<li><a href="http://www.lib.muohio.edu/multifacet/books/' . $data
    ->$bibkeys->subjects[$i]->name . '?field=subjects">' . $data->$bibkeys
    ->subjects[$i]->name . '</a></li>';
}
print '</ul>';
print '<p>Download:</p>';
print '<ul>';
?>
```

OPEN LIBRARY COVERS API

The Open Library Books API returns a lot of data. Some or most of that data may not be of interest to you. It would be overkill to use the Books API if you are interested only in book covers. For that, we would use the Open Library Covers API. This short example will cycle through an array of ISBNs and print out the matching covers.

First, let's take a look at the base URL request form and the parameters for the Covers API.

The base URL:

```
http://covers.openlibrary.org/b/
```

The parameters:

PARAMETER	MEANING	REQUIRED
ID	ID used to search Open Library Covers; API accepts ISBN, LCCN, OCLC number, OLID (Open Library ID), and Cover ID	Yes
ID value	The value of the ID (i.e., an ISBN)	Yes
Sizes	Specifies what size of cover you want returned; S, M, and L are the accepted values	Yes

What is slightly different about this API is that the parameter names are not actually put into the URL, only the values of the parameters. So, for example, a fully formed Covers API URL would be

```
http://covers.openlibrary.org/b/isbn/0553103547-M.jpg
```

These elements must be added in this order. After the base URL place the ID type on which you will be searching (e.g., ISBN or LCCN, etc.). Next, place the actual value of the ID type (e.g., the ISBN number). Finally, append -M.jpg to the end of the ID number. The value M signifies medium. Use -S.jpg or -L.jpg for small or large. (These values are case-sensitive.)

Let's see the API in action.

OPEN LIBRARY COVERS API IN ACTION

This brief example will cycle through an array of ISBNs and print out their accompanying covers. Note that this is a better of way of utilizing Open Library's API if you only need covers. Using the Books API would return too much superfluous data.

Create a new file in your text editor and let's get started:

```php
<?php
$ids = array ("0" => "0553103547", "1" => "0553108034", "2" => "055357342X");
```

This line above is creating an array of ISBNs upon which we can iteratively work. It is not likely that you would hand-code ISBNs this way. Most likely, if you have access to your catalog, the ISBNs are already stored as an array item. This example, however, will illustrate how this can be done. The next lines of our script are

```php
$id = "isbn";
$url = "http://covers.openlibrary.org/b/";
$count = count($isbns);
```

Here we are setting a few variables. First, we have $id, which is initially set to equal isbn. This is the variable you would change to search on different ID types. The next variable $url is our base URL. Finally, we have a count of all the ISBNs in our array to use in our subsequent for loop:

```php
for ($i = 0; $i < $count; $i++) {
$ids[$i] .= "-M.jpg";
```

What this line within the for loop is doing is appending -M.jpg to each ISBN to turn it into a functioning file name to be used in when we print out the URL as an image source:

```php
print "<img src=" . $url . "" . $ids[$i] . " />";
}
```

Essentially what we are doing here is attaching two variables together to form the proper URL request:

```php
$url (http://covers.openlibrary.org/b/isbn/) + $ids[$i] (0553103547-M.jpg) =
      http://covers.openlibrary.org/b/isbn/0553103547-M.jpg
```

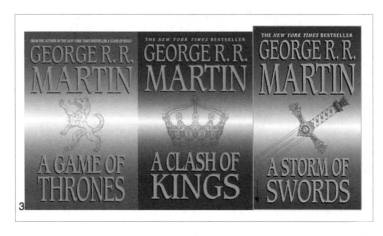

Here's the full script:

```php
<?php
$ids = array ("0" => "0553103547", "1" => "0553108034", "2" => "055357342X");
$id = "isbn";
$count = count($ids);
echo $count;
$url = "http://covers.openlibrary.org/b/$id/";
for ($i = 0; $i < $count; $i++) {
$ids[$i] .= "-M.jpg";
print "<img src=" . $url . "" . $ids[$i] . " />";
}
?>
```

CHAPTER EIGHT

LIBRARYTHING API AND LIBRARIES

LibraryThing is a web-based cataloging system that allows individuals to catalog their own book collections. LibraryThing is connected to the Library of Congress, Amazon.com, and nearly 700 libraries around the world. So users aren't so much hand-keying bibliographic records as pulling in that data from other sources. It's very similar to Open Library in that it is a wiki-like concept. However, there are some distinctions. First, Open Library is a free service, and its goal is to create a web-based catalog of every book ever published; it's not a tool to catalog one's personal collections. Second, the data that you can get from Open Library is a bit limited as opposed to LibraryThing. LibraryThing, on the other hand, is a fee-based service.

LibraryThing offers several APIs:

- **Web Services API.** This API gets you the basic bibliographic information as well as supplementary and value-added content. It requires a developer key. The Web Services API is the primary reason to utilize LibraryThing, especially if you're a developer. It returns information such as awards a book has received, important places mentioned in the book, important character names mentioned, and also first and last lines.
- **Covers API.** This API allows you to capture cover images, much like the Open Library API. It requires a developer key.
- **ThingISBN.** This API works in much the same way as WorldCat's xISBN service. Supply it with an ISBN, and the API will return related ISBNs.

LIBRARYTHING WEB SERVICES API TECHNICAL DETAILS

There are two flavors of the Web Services API: a method that returns detailed bibliographic information (librarything.ck.getwork) and another that returns author information (librarything.ck.getauthor). These APIs require a developer key, which can be obtained free of charge from LibraryThing.

Both methods work like many of the other APIs we've looked at in this book, relying on a simple HTTP GET or POST action. The base URL request format is

```
http://www.librarything.com/services/rest/1.1/?
```

Like the other APIs, this API depends upon parameters and values being appended to the URL. LibraryThing only has three parameters:

PARAMETER	MEANING	REQUIRED
method	Determines the data that will be returned: book or author	Yes
type	The type of numerical data to search for; supported numbers are LibraryThing ID and ISBN	Yes
apikey	Your API developer key	Yes

These APIs return data in the REST response format (XML) only. The XML tree that it returns is fairly complex and unfortunately of an inconsistent structure that requires a bit more programming. We'll take a step-by-step look at this.

LIBRARYTHING WEB SERVICES API IN ACTION

Before we get started in the script, let's take a look at the type of data being returned and what the XML format looks like. Open up your web browser and place this into your URL space:

```
http://www.librarything.com/services/rest/1.1/?method=librarything.ck.getwork&
    isbn=0316017922&apikey=your_developer_key
```

You should see an XML document that looks similar to this:

```
<response stat="ok">
 <ltml xmlns="http://www.librarything.com/" version="1.1">
```

```
<item id="5394345" type="work">
   <author id="185" authorcode="gladwellmalcolm">Malcolm Gladwell</author>
   <url>http://www.librarything.com/work/5394345</url>
   <commonknowledge>
    <fieldList>
      <field type="41" name="originaltitle" displayName="Original title">
        <versionList>
          <version id="3937937" archived="0" lang="eng">
            <date timestamp="1311096070">Tue, 19 Jul 2011 13:21:10 -0400
            </date>
            <person id="1086705">
               <name>Maikall</name>
               <url>http://www.librarything.com/profile/Maikall</url>
            </person>
            <factList>
               <fact>Outliers</fact>
            </factList>
          </version>
        </versionList>
      </field>
```

This XML file continues with several `<field></field>` sections, each of which gives us a particular type of data about the book at hand. For this API in Action section we will extract the title, author, and interesting supplementary data such as important places, awards, and character names. After you run through this example, take a look at the XML and pull out the data that you are interested in.

Create a new PHP file on your web server and let's get started with this API. Remember that this API requires the use of three parameters: method, id type and value, and developer key. Let's declare those values as variables to start:

```
<?php
$key = "1a4521f53828296837ea0d9b3d5997b2";
$method = "librarything.ck.getwork";
$type = "isbn";
$id = "0316017922";
```

Recall that `librarything.ck.getwork` will return information about the book rather than about the author.

For this example use my values for `$method`, `$type` and `$id`. You will need to acquire your own API key. Let's continue by declaring the variable for our URL:

```
$url = "http://www.librarything.com/services/rest/1.1/?";
$url .= "method=$method";
$url .= "&$type=$id";
$url .= "&apikey=$key";
```

Again, what we are doing here is first declaring the `$url`. The base URL is what appears first. The following three `$url` declarations are the values that will be appended to the end of the original variable. Before continuing on, echo out your `$url` variable to ensure that the variable has been concatenated properly:

```
echo $url;
```

Open your browser and pull up this PHP script. You should see the URL request format with the parameters appended to the end so that it looks like this:

```
http://www.librarything.com/services/rest/1.1/?method=librarything.ck.getwork&
    isbn=0316017922&apikey=your_developer_key
```

Continuing the script: because we are working with an XML response, we will need to employ the use of cURL, as we did with the WorldCat Basic API. First, we initialize the cURL session, with the understanding that the data will be pulled from the `$url` variable:

```
$ch = curl_init($url);
```

Next, we set our cURL options:

```
curl_setopt($ch, CURLOPT_RETURNTRANSFER, true);
curl_setopt($ch, CURLOPT_HEADER, 0);
```

Then we execute the cURL session and store the returned data in the `$data` variable.

```
$data = curl_exec($ch);
```

Finally, we close the cURL session;

```
curl_close($ch);
```

Let's take a look at `$data` to note the difference between this data and what is returned when we go to the request URL in the browser.

```
echo htmlentities($data);
```

What you should see is a big block of HTML. There isn't much we can do to parse this with PHP at this point.

The next line of the script takes the raw data in `$data` and transforms it into SimpleXML format to enable us to parse it.

```
$doc = new SimpleXmlElement($data);
```

Now take a look at `$doc` by executing a `print_r` on it:

```
print '<pre>';
print_r ($doc);
print '</pre>';
```

What is returned should be more recognizable to you: an array we can now parse to begin pulling out our desired data.

Here the script is going to get a bit more complicated than our previous examples. The reason for this is that LibraryThing is giving us an inconsistent XML tree for each book. Take a look at the array that you just executed a `print_r` to see. Find the `[field]` array. It is couched two levels within the `[commonknowledge]` object (about 26 lines down). Each field within this array contains data about a specific aspect of the book. For example, the first field (index number 0), indicated by `[0]`, contains the "original title." You can see this in the `[@attributes]` array.

Scrolling further down the page the next item in the array (index number 1), `[1]`, is about "media reviews." Find the data that we are interested in pulling out—namely, `awards`, `placesmentioned`, and `characternames`—and note their particular index numbers. You'll see that `awards` is index number 9; `placesmentioned` is 7; and `characternames` is 10.

If each XML tree for each book returned via the API used these same index numbers, then the script would be straightforward; but alas the index numbers are different for each book. To test this, replace the ISBN that we have in the script for *Outliers* with the ISBN for *A Game of Thrones* (0553573403). Remember that all you need to do to accomplish this is go to the `$id` variable near the top of the script and replace the ISBN.

Now when you take a look at the returned data in the browser, note the index numbers for those same three fields. They're different, aren't they? Thus we need to add a little bit more PHP logic to straighten this out and always return the desired data, regardless of ISBN. The one thing that does remain consistent is the names of the fields. For each book the field for character names is `characternames`; the field for important places is `placesmentioned`. We will use this fact to figure out the exact index number, which is necessary to print out the corresponding data.

First, we create a variable for the `[field]` array in question:

```
$array = $doc->ltml->item->commonknowledge->fieldList;
```

Next, we'll tabulate the number of index numbers in the array to use in a `for` loop that I will introduce in a moment.

```
$count = count($doc->ltml->item->commonknowledge->fieldList->children());
```

Then we create a variable for each one of the individual fields. You will see how this comes into play next.

```
$value = $array->field;
```

Next, we start our `for` loop.

```
for ($i = 0; $i < $count; $i++) {
```

For each index number we will execute the following:

```
if ($value[$i]['name'] == "canonicaltitle") {
```

Thanks to the consistency of the data, we haven't needed to employ this kind of PHP logic in any of our other examples. Essentially this line is saying that if the name of the field is "canonicaltitle" then do the following, which is to create a variable that we will print out:

```
$title = $doc->ltml->item->commonknowledge->fieldList->field[$i]->versionList
    ->version->factList->fact;
```

The `$i` is important here. It is the index number. It ensures that our `$title` variable will contain the title. So if the index number for `canonicaltitle` is 5 in the XML of one book and 3 in another, `$title` will always return the title and not something else.

```
print '<h1>' . $title . '</h1>';
    }
}
```

Be sure to include the correct number of closing curly brackets.

Test this out. Go to your browser and load the PHP file. You should see the title of the book in question. The true test however is to change the ISBN. Do that and check again. You should see the title. It worked!

The author field doesn't require any of this additional logic, since it's not in that `[field]` array. It's always under `[item]`. So to print out the author, all we need to do is this:

```
print '<h2>' . $doc->ltml->item->author . '</h2>';
```

Let's finish this script and print out awards, important places, and character names using the same `if` logic. However, there is one additional layer of complexity, which is that each of those fields may have multiple values. *Outliers*, for example, has won numerous awards and mentions various places and characters. This will require us to embed an additional `for` loop within our main `for` loop. Continuing with the script, let's get the count on the number of items in the `$awards` array:

```
for ($i = 0; $i < $count; $i++) {
if ($value[$i]['name'] == "awards") {
$awards = $doc->ltml->item->commonknowledge->fieldList->field[$i]->versionList
    ->version->factList->fact;
$awards_count = count($awards);
```

Next comes our new embedded `for` loop, which is looping through the awards and printing them out:

```
print '<h3>Awards</h3>';
for ($j = 0; $j < $awards_count; $j++) {
echo $awards[$j] . '<br />';
}
print '<br />';
}
```

The process for places and characters is exactly the same:

```
if ($value[$i]['name'] == "placesmentioned") {
$places = $doc->ltml->item->commonknowledge->fieldList->field[$i]->versionList
    ->version->factList->fact;
$places_count = count($places);
print '<h3>Important Places</h3>';
for ($h = 0; $h < $places_count; $h++) {
echo $places[$h] . '<br />';
}
print '<br />';
}
if ($value[$i]['name'] == "characternames") {
$names = $doc->ltml->item->commonknowledge->fieldList->field[$i]->versionList
    ->version->factList->fact;
$names_count = count($names);
print '<h3>Character Names</h3>';
for ($g = 0; $g < $names_count; $g++) {
echo $names[$g] . '<br />';
}
}
}
```

A Game of Thrones

George R. R. Martin

Character Names

Eddard "Ned" Stark
Catelyn Tully Stark
Brandon "Bran" Stark
Sansa Stark
Arya Stark
Jon Snow
Tyrion Lannister
Daenerys "Dany" Targaryen
Cersei Lannister
Robert Baratheon
Joffrey Baratheon
Jaime Lannister
Robb Stark
Petyr Baelish "Littlefinger"
Stannis Baratheon
Sandor Clegane
Rickon Stark
Hodor
Benjen Stark
Daeren Targaryen
Khal Drogo
Gared
Waymar Royce
Maester Aemon
Mance Rayder

Here's the complete script:

```php
<?php
$key = "your_key_here";
$method = "librarything.ck.getwork";
$type = "isbn";
$id = "0553573403";
$url = "http://www.librarything.com/services/rest/1.1/?";
$url .= "method=$method";
$url .= "&$type=$id";
$url .= "&apikey=$key";
$ch = curl_init($url);
curl_setopt($ch, CURLOPT_RETURNTRANSFER, true);
curl_setopt($ch, CURLOPT_HEADER, 0);
$data = curl_exec($ch);
curl_close($ch);
echo $url;
$doc = new SimpleXmlElement($data);
$array = $doc->ltml->item->commonknowledge->fieldList;
$count = count($doc->ltml->item->commonknowledge->fieldList->children());
$value = $array->field;
for ($i = 0; $i < $count; $i++) {
if ($value[$i]['name'] == "canonicaltitle") {
$title = $doc->ltml->item->commonknowledge->fieldList->field[$i]->versionList
        ->version->factList->fact;
print '<h1>' . $title . '</h1>';
}
}
```

```php
print '<h2>' . $doc->ltml->item->author . '</h2>';
for ($i = 0; $i < $count; $i++) {
if ($value[$i]['name'] == "awards") {
$awards = $doc->ltml->item->commonknowledge->fieldList->field[$i]->versionList
       ->version->factList->fact;
$awards_count = count($awards);
print '<h3>Awards</h3>';
for ($j = 0; $j < $awards_count; $j++) {
echo $awards[$j] . '<br />';
}
print '<br />';
}
if ($value[$i]['name'] == "placesmentioned") {
$places = $doc->ltml->item->commonknowledge->fieldList->field[$i]->versionList
       ->version->factList->fact;
$places_count = count($places);
print '<h3>Important Places</h3>';
for ($h = 0; $h < $places_count; $h++) {
echo $places[$h] . '<br />';
}
print '<br />';
}
if ($value[$i]['name'] == "characternames") {
$names = $doc->ltml->item->commonknowledge->fieldList->field[$i]->versionList
       ->version->factList->fact;
$names_count = count($names);
print '<h3>Character Names</h3>';
for ($g = 0; $g < $names_count; $g++) {
echo $names[$g] . '<br />';
}
}
}
?>
```

CHAPTER NINE

GOODREADS API AND LIBRARIES

Goodreads.com is a social web service for book lovers that is very similar to Library-Thing. Goodreads offers developers a wide-ranging set of APIs, with the goal of creating and maintaining a rich developer community to build up the site's popularity through third-party apps. Much of the data and functionality that is offered through the API falls outside of the scope of most libraries' missions, but it does offer one type of content that no other service that we've talked about provides—reviews.

According to Goodreads, they have more than 10 million reviews across 700,000 titles—not an insignificant amount. This type of data is very rich and can add value to your catalog display.

GOODREADS API TECHNICAL DETAILS

The Goodreads API requires a developer key. To get a key, first create a Goodreads account at www.goodreads.com/user/new then obtain a developer key at www.goodreads.com/api/keys.

Goodreads offers nearly fifty APIs to build robust third-party applications. We will be taking a look at and utilizing two of these APIs.

Goodreads ISBN to ID API

The ISBN to ID API is very simple. It supports HTTP GET requests only.

The base URL request format for this API is

```
http://www.goodreads.com/book/isbn_to_id?
```

Appended to this base URL are two required parameters:

PARAMETER	MEANING	REQUIRED
isbn	ISBN of the item in question	Yes
key	Your API developer key	Yes

Adding these parameters will result in a properly constructed URL that will look like this:

```
http://www.goodreads.com/book/isbn_to_id?isbn=0553573403&key=your_key
```

Type this URL into your browser and see what you get back. What you should see is the Goodreads ID as plain text in your browser. It couldn't be more simple.

Goodreads Review API

The Goodreads Review API offers more than 10 million reviews across 700,000 titles. Utilizing this API has the potential to add value to your catalog and website.

Unfortunately, the API returns a preformatted HTML iframe (inline frame) widget (either embedded within JSON or XML). Styling and formatting the reviews to fit your aesthetic is not possible, though the widget itself is attractive and functional.

The base URL request format for this API is

```
http://www.goodreads.com/book/show?
```

There are several potential parameters for this API:

PARAMETER	MEANING	REQUIRED
id	Goodreads ID; obtained from ISBN to ID API	Yes
key	Your API developer key	Yes

format	Format of returned data: XML or JSON	No
rating	Show reviews with a certain rating	No
text_only	Only display reviews with text; defaults to false	No

A properly constructed URL will look like this:

```
http://www.goodreads.com/book/show?format=json&key=your_key&id=409207
```

If you put this URL in your browser you should see the iframe widget embedded in JSON notation:

```
{"reviews_widget":"<style>\n  #goodreads-widget {\n    font-family: georgia,
serif;\n    padding: 18px 0;\n    width:565px;\n  }\n  #goodreads-widget h1
{\n    font-weight:normal;\n    font-size: 16px;\n    border-bottom: 1px
solid #BBB596;\n    margin-bottom: 0;\n  }\n  #goodreads-widget a {\n    text
-decoration: none;\n    color:#660;\n  }\n  iframe{\n    background-color:
#fff;\n  }\n  #goodreads-widget a:hover { text-decoration: underline;
}\n  #goodreads-widget a:active {\n    color:#660;\n  }\n  #gr_footer {\n
width: 100%;\n    border-top: 1px solid #BBB596;\n    text-align: right;\n
}\n  #goodreads-widget .gr_branding{\n    color: #382110;\n    font-size:
11px;\n    text-decoration: none;\n    font-family: verdana, arial, helvetica,
sans-serif;\n  }\n</style>\n<div id=\"goodreads-widget\">\n  <div id=\"gr_
header\"><h1><a href=\"http://www.goodreads.com/book/show/409207
.A_Game_of_Thrones\">A Game of Thrones Reviews</a></h1></div>\n  <iframe
id=\"the_iframe\" src=\"http://www.goodreads.com/api/reviews_widget_
iframe?did=DEVELOPER_ID&amp;isbn=0553573403&amp;links=660&amp;review_
back=fff&amp;text=000\" width=\"565\" height=\"400\" frameborder=\"0\">
</iframe>\n  <div id=\"gr_footer\">\n    <a href=\"http://www.goodreads.com
/book/show/409207.A_Game_of_Thrones?utm_medium=api&amp;utm_source=reviews_
widget\" class=\"gr_branding\" target=\"_blank\">Reviews from Goodreads.com
</a>\n  </div>\n</div>\n"}
```

Now that we grasp the basic technical details of these two particular APIs, let's put them into action.

GOODREADS REVIEWS API IN ACTION

For this review-grabbing application we will employ the use of two APIs in one script. First we will use the Goodreads ISBN to ID API to get the proper Goodreads ID for use in the Review API.

Let's get started by declaring some of our variables:

```php
<?php
$k = "your_key_here";
$isbn = "0553573403";
```

Remember that you will need to obtain an API key for this script. Replace "your_key_here" with your API key. For the $isbn variable, use this example for now. This variable can be dynamically created depending on how it's integrated into your catalog.

Now, since the Reviews API requires a Goodreads ID, we will need to obtain that ID through the ISBN to ID API.

```php
$id_url = "http://www.goodreads.com/book/isbn_to_id";
```

This is the base request URL format, onto which we will concatenate the parameters that we declared as our variables above:

```php
$id_url .= "?isbn=$isbn";
$id_url .= "&key=$k";
```

To check for URL accuracy, echo your $id_url:

```php
echo $id_url;
```

This is what you should see when you point your browser to this script:

> http://www.goodreads.com/book/isbn_to_id?isbn=0553573403&key
> =your_key

Now that our URL is properly formatted, we can use it to extract data from the API. Again, this API is very simple and returns only the Goodreads ID as a plain text string. So we can put that string into a variable to use later:

```php
$gid = file_get_contents($id_url);
```

To ensure that you have the correct data, echo out $gid:

```php
echo $gid;
```

You should see nothing but the Goodreads ID echoed out to the browser. Since it is stored in a variable, we can use it with the Goodreads Review API. Let's continue. First, we need to declare our format variable and then declare a variable for the base URL request format:

```
$format = "json";
$review_url = "http://www.goodreads.com/book/show";
```

Next, we need to concatenate our parameters onto the base `$review_url` variable.

```
$review_url .= "?format=$format";
$review_url .= "&key=$k";
$review_url .= "&id=$gid";
```

This last concatenation is placing the Goodreads ID obtained earlier in the script onto the request URL.

Again, you should `echo` out the `$review_url` to ensure that everything is correct before proceeding. If the URL is not constructed properly, the data will not be received from Goodreads.

```
echo $review_url;
```

You should see the following URL echoed out in your browser:

> http://www.goodreads.com/book/show?format=json&key=your
> _key&id=409207

Once our URL is constructed correctly, we can move on to the data retrieval and parsing section of the script:

```
$raw_data = file_get_contents($review_url);
```

This line of code pulls the data returned from `$review_url` and places it in the variable `$raw_data`, which is in JSON format. Thus we need to decode the JSON:

```
$data = json_decode($raw_data);
```

Now our data is stored in a PHP object and is easily obtainable. To see the data you have to work with (which in the case of this API is only one PHP object, which has the reviews widget embedded), do a `print_r` on the `$data` variable:

```
print '<pre>';
print_r ($data);
print '</pre>';
```

What you'll see when you print out this variable is a PHP object and the embedded review widget:

```
stdClass Object
(
[reviews_widget] =>
```

```
)
```

Since we want to display only the widget and not the encapsulating PHP object, we'll need to place the widget in a variable and then print that out within HTML:

```
$reviews = $data->reviews_widget;
```

Now, we can utilize the widget in any web application we'd like. Simply print out the `$reviews` variable:

```
print '<p>' . $reviews . '</p>';
```

```
http://www.goodreads.com/book/isbn_to_id?isbn=0553573403&key=hvibjxxA2W02eyHFQYYVmA
http://www.goodreads.com/book/show?format=json&key=hvibjxxA2W02eyHFQYYVmA&id=409207
```

A Game of Thrones Reviews

[Write a review] (you'll need to sign in to your Goodreads account or sign up)   (showing 1-6 of 10,114)

By Keely (Belleville, NJ) · 1 of 5 stars · March 02, 2010

There are plenty of fantasy authors who claim to be doing something different with the genre.
Ironically, they often write the most predictable books of all, as evidenced by Goodkind and
Paolini. Though I'm not sure why they protest so much; predictability is rarely a death sentence in
genre fantasy ...more

By Shannon (Toronto, Canada) · 1 of 5 stars · May 25, 2008

I really feel the necessity of a bit of personal backstory here, before I start the review. Back in
1996 when this book first came out, and I was about 14 or 16 years old, I saw the hardcover on a
sale table for about $5 and couldn't resist a bargain (still can't, though I'm more cautious these
days ...more

By Anila (The United States) · 1 of 5 stars · February 03, 2012

WARNING: If you enjoyed this book, even a little bit, you may not want to read this review. It will
probably make you angry. Heaven knows that the book made *me* furious, and I intend to turn
every bit of that wrath back on it.
Instead, I suggest you read karen's review, Aerin's review, Joyzi's ...more

Reviews from Goodreads.com

Here's the complete script:

```php
<?php
$k = "your_key_here";
$isbn = "0553573403";
// Get Goodreads ID via ISBN //
$id_url = "http://www.goodreads.com/book/isbn_to_id";
$id_url .= "?isbn=$isbn";
$id_url .= "&key=$k";
$gid = file_get_contents($id_url);
// Get Reviews via $gid //
$format = "json";
$review_url = "http://www.goodreads.com/book/show";
$review_url .= "?format=$format";
$review_url .= "&key=$k";
$review_url .= "&id=$gid";
$raw_data = file_get_contents($review_url);
$data = json_decode($raw_data);
$reviews = $data->reviews_widget;
echo $id_url;
print '<br />';
echo $review_url;
print '<p>' . $reviews . '</p>';
```

CHAPTER TEN

GOOGLE BOOKS API AND LIBRARIES

The Google Books API offers access to Google's vast library of book data, including metadata, covers, downloadable e-book formats, and an embeddable e-book viewer. Libraries can add value and functionality to their catalogs by utilizing the Google Books API.

We will examine the API by running a search for a known item and returning its metadata and links to any available previews or downloadable content; we will run a search on a subject and display the results; and we will print out Google's embeddable e-book viewer.

GOOGLE BOOKS API TECHNICAL DETAILS

The Google Books API allows data extraction via HTTP requests and returns data primarily in JSON format. The embeddable e-book viewer works via simple JavaScript, which we will delve into later. All applications using the API require a Google account and developer key, which can be obtained at https://code.google .com/apis/console.

We will use the Google Books Search API to return book data on simple queries; however, Google offers many more APIs for more advanced applications.

The base URL request format is

```
https://www.googleapis.com/books/v1/volumes?q=
```

Google being Google, there are several parameters and search filters you can add to your search to return the most relevant data.

PARAMETER	MEANING	REQUIRED

q	Search query using keywords; special keywords can be added to search string to search within certain fields:
	`intitle:`
	`inauthor:`
	`inpublisher:`
	`subject:`
	`isbn:`
	`lccn:`
	`oclc:`
		Yes; special keywords not required

key	Your API developer key	Yes
download	Returns only results with downloadable content available; `epub` is the only accepted value	No

filter	Refines results by availability of book; accepted values:
	`partial` (at least partial preview)
	`full` (only full book)
	`free-ebooks`
	`paid-ebooks`
	`ebooks` (paid or free)
		No

startIndex	Where to start returning list of results	No
maxResults	Maximum number of results to return; default is 10, max is 40	No

printType	Refines results by publication type; accepted values:
	`all`
	`books`
	`magazines`
		No

orderBy	Results can be sorted by `relevance` or `newest`	No

GOOGLE BOOKS API IN ACTION

Searching for and Displaying a Known Item

Create a new PHP file and save it to your web server. To start using the Google Books API, we need to declare a few variables:

```
$k = "your_key_here";
$isbn = "0553573403";
$url = "https://www.googleapis.com/books/v1/volumes?q=";
```

The variable `$k` is the developer key you obtained from Google Developers. And since in this example we are searching for a known item, we are putting the ISBN in the variable `$isbn`. After that is our base URL request format.

To keep things simple for this first example, let's not add any other parameters such as `filter` or `orderBy`.

We have our base URL, but we need to concatenate the ISBN search query. Remember that Google offers special keywords to search in certain fields. Since we are searching for an ISBN we can use the `isbn:` search keyword:

```
$url .= "isbn:$isbn";
```

Before we proceed let's add our developer key:

```
$url .= "&key=$k";
```

Let's echo out our URL to ensure we have it constructed properly before continuing:

```
echo $url;
```

Open your browser and open up your PHP file; you should see a long URL request string printed out:

> https://www.googleapis.com/books/v1/volumes?q=isbn:0553573403&
> key=your_key

If you copy that URL and paste it into a new tab in your browser, you will see the JSON data structure that Google is returning:

```json
{
"kind": "books#volumes",
"totalItems": 1,
"items": [
    {
        "kind": "books#volume",
        "id": "btpIkZ6X6egC",
        "etag": "I7YcM59I48c",
        "selfLink": "https://www.googleapis.com/books/v1/volumes/btpIkZ6X6egC",
        "volumeInfo": {
         "title": "A game of thrones",
         "authors": [
           "George R. R. Martin"
         ],
         "publisher": "Spectra",
         "publishedDate": "1997-08-04",
         "description": "The kingdom of the royal Stark family faces its ultimate
         challenge in the onset of a generation-long winter, the poisonous plots
         of the rival Lannisters, the . . .",
         "industryIdentifiers": [
           {
             "type": "ISBN_10",
             "identifier": "0553573403"
           },
           {
             "type": "ISBN_13",
             "identifier": "9780553573404"
           }
         ] . . .
    }
```

As we've seen with other APIs, dealing with JSON is relatively straightforward. We need to perform a few PHP functions to get the data into easily parsed PHP arrays:

```php
$raw_data = file_get_contents($url);
$data = json_decode($raw_data);
```

The returned JSON data is now available as a PHP object stored in `$data`. To see that data, simply wrap it in `<pre>` tags and perform a `print_r` on the variable:

```php
print '<pre>';
print_r ($data);
print '</pre>';
```

Open up your browser to see the output. It is a useful exercise to compare the differences in the data structure between this PHP object and the JSON data structure that Google provides.

Now that we have the data in PHP, it's ready to be parsed. There are several pieces of data that would be useful for libraries to display in a catalog or other web application. We can print out the title, author, publisher, cover image, and also a link to the preview of the work in question. This could be especially valuable to library users, since Google offers very generous previews. Many times, especially in academic library settings, users only need access to a certain chapter or number of pages. Linking to a large preview of the work could be just what the patron needs.

To continue, let's print out the cover image. If you take a look in the PHP object you will see that there are two URLs that point to cover images. They are within the `imageLinks` object, which is embedded in the `volumeInfo` object. Before we print out the cover image, we can put the URL to the image in a variable:

```
$img_src = "$data->items[0]->volumeInfo->imageLinks->thumbnail"
```

Now that it's in a variable, we can print it out:

```
print '<img src="' . $img_src . '" />';
```

Double-check that your quotes are correct for the above `print` command. With HTML the source URL following `img src=` needs to be in double quotes. To place a PHP variable within the double quotes, use bookending single quotes and periods, like this:

```
' . $variable . '
```

Now that we have the cover image printed out, let's print out the title, author, and publisher. As we did with the cover image, we can place this data in a variable first:

```
$title = $data->items[0]->volumeInfo->title;
$author = $data->items[0]->volumeInfo->authors[0];
$publisher = $data->items[0]->volumeInfo->publisher;
```

Now that we have the data in simple, portable variables we can wrap them in HTML:

```
print '<h2>' . $title . '</h2>';
print '<h3>' . $author . '</h3>';
print '<h4>' . $publisher . '</h4>';
```

Save your file and open it up in your browser. You should see a layout similar to this:

While this is useful, the value that Google Books offers is in the previews of the books they have in their collection. We can provide links to Google's interface so users can read the preview. The URL to the book preview is contained within `previewLink` in the `volumeInfo` object. As with the other data, let's put this URL into a portable variable:

```
$preview = $data->items[0]->volumeInfo->previewLink;
```

Wrap this variable in HTML to transform it into a hyperlink:

```
print '<a href="' . $preview . '">Read the Preview</a>';
```

Save your file and open it in your browser and you should see a hyperlink that when clicked takes you to Google Book's interface, allowing you to read the preview.

The Google Books API, however, makes it even more convenient for us to connect our users with its content—via its embeddable Google Books Viewer. Rather than merely linking users to the preview content, we can embed a viewer on our pages so the user can view the content immediately. This is achieved through some basic JavaScript.

Let's work within the same script that we've been writing. Open up the file in your text editor and find a spot in the file before it contains any HTML. We need to print out HTML header information and include a JavaScript file in the `<head>` section.

Right before you print out the cover image, type the following:

```
print '<!DOCTYPE html PUBLIC "-//W3C//DTD XHTML 1.0 Transitional//EN" "http://
    www.w3.org/TR/xhtml1/DTD/xhtml1-transitional.dtd">';
print '<html>
    <head>
    <meta http-equiv="content-type" content="text/html; charset=utf-8" />
    <title>Google Book API Example</title>
    <script type="text/javascript" src="//www.google.com/jsapi"></script>
    <script type="text/javascript">
    google.load("books", "0", {"language" : "pt-EN"});
    function initialize() {
        var viewer = new google.books.DefaultViewer(document.getElementById
        (\'viewerCanvas\'));
        viewer.load(\'ISBN:' . $isbn . '\');
    }
    google.setOnLoadCallback(initialize);
    </script>';
print '</head>';
```

We need to embed the JavaScript in an HTML head section, so it's best to declare a DOCTYPE and make sure our page is XHTML compliant. There are a couple of JavaScript files in play here. The first is external and contained in a link (www.google.com/jsapi). The second is internal and is also contained in the `<head>` section of our HTML. The JavaScript needs an ISBN to work properly, so we can supply it with our ISBN. Since we have our ISBN saved in a variable, it is easy for us to drop that variable into the JavaScript notation:

```
viewer.load(\'ISBN:' . $isbn . '\');
```

All that we need to do now is to display the viewer signified on this line of JavaScript code:

```
var viewer = new google.books.DefaultViewer(document.getElementById(\'viewer
    Canvas\'));
```

What is important here is `viewerCanvas`. Because that is the name of the div ID that we will need in order to launch the viewer.

Place this line of code after the `<head>` section:

```
print '<div id="viewerCanvas" style="width: 600px; height: 500px"></div>';
```

Save the file and open it in a browser, and you should now see the embedded viewer.

Adopting this technique and implementing the Google Books viewer on the detailed record view in your catalog would be an excellent way to add value to your users' experience.

Both of these examples assumed a known item. The Google Books API will also allow you to run searches and pull data out for subject or keyword searches.

Let's build a script that runs both a keyword and a subject search and that will also incorporate some of the several parameters the Google Books API includes.

Let's start from scratch on a new PHP script and begin by declaring our variables:

```php
<?php
$k = "your_key";
$q = urlencode("coffee");
$url = "https://www.googleapis.com/books/v1/volumes?q=";
$url .= "$q";
$url .= "&key=$k";
```

Instead of searching on an ISBN, we are searching for the keyword "coffee." The keyword or keywords immediately follow the q= in the URL request string, which is why we have the $q variable concatenated to $url.

Test the construction of your URL by using the echo command on the $url variable:

```
echo $url;
```

If constructed correctly, the URL should look like this:

https://www.googleapis.com/books/v1/volumes?q=coffee&key=your_key

Test this URL before proceeding with the script by copying it into the URL bar of your browser.

A properly constructed request URL will return JSON data in the browser. If you see this data, then we can proceed with the script:

```
$raw_data = file_get_contents($url);
$data = json_decode($raw_data);
```

As we've seen in other scripts, these two lines first grab the data from Google and then decode the JSON and translate it into a PHP object stored in the $data variable.

It is good practice and also helps with scripting to print out this PHP object to see how it's constructed:

```
print '<pre>';
print_r ($data);
print '</pre>';
```

Opening the file in your browser will display the PHP object and allow you to see its architecture. Please take special note of the second field in the array `total Items`. When we change our query to a subject search you should see that number decrease a bit.

Since we are dealing with more than one returned book record, we need to incorporate a `for` loop into our script to print the relevant data for each book:

```
for ($i = 0; $i < $count; $i++) {
```

This line starts our `for` loop. For a detailed explanation of PHP `for` loops, please review the PHP concepts in the Technical Primer section of the introduction.

Now for each book record let's print out the cover image, title, authors, and description, as well as links to the preview and any available downloadable ePubs or PDFs.

We are currently in the `for` loop, so for each book we will do the following:

```
print '<img src="' . $data->items[$i]->volumeInfo->imageLinks->thumbnail . '"
    />';
print '<h2>' . $data->items[$i]->volumeInfo->title . '</h2>';
```

In the first line here we are wrapping the URL of the cover image in an HTML image source tag to print out the image. Secondly, we are wrapping the title in `<h2>` header tags. To get an idea of what this looks like, go ahead and close out the `for` loop with a curly bracket:

```
}
```

Go to your browser and see how everything looks. You should see cover images followed by titles of the books. To continue with the script, reopen the `for` loop by deleting the closing curly bracket.

The next piece of data that we will print out is the author or authors. Now this part will be a little tricky because for each book there is either one author or more than one author. We need to account for that potentiality by including some `if` logic to determine whether there are multiple authors and if so, we need to embed another `for` loop to print out each author.

In order to print out the authors, we need to do a couple of things. First, we will place the path to the author array in an easily portable variable:

```
$authors = $data->items[$i]->volumeInfo->authors;
```

Next, we need to get a count on the number of items in the author array to use in our embedded `for` loop:

```
$acount = count($authors);
```

What we are going to do is print out the authors in an HTML paragraph with a comma separating each author. This is a bit more complicated than you may imagine at first, because there are two different potentialities: one is that there is one author, in which case we will not need to print out a comma or blank space; the other possibility is that there is more than one author, which could mean two or more, in which case we need to print out a comma and a space between each author *except* after the last author.

First, we need to get the count of the number of authors:

```
$acount = count($authors);
$lcount = ($acount-1);
```

We will use this in our subsequent `for` loop. The variable `$lcount` is the index number of the last author in the author array. We need to get this number because we will print this author without a comma following it.

Continuing with the script, we need to print out our opening paragraph tag. All of the authors will be printed out within one paragraph.

```
print '<p>';
```

Next is the logic for situations where there is more than one author:

```
if ($acount > 1) {
 for ($j = 0; $j < $acount; $j++) {
```

This sets up the `for` loop for those author arrays with more than one author. Since the last author that we print out is unique in that it must not be followed by a comma and a space, we need to do some more logic to separate it out and print it out differently.

To start with, we'll use a new variable that will come into play in a moment:

```
$a2 = $j-1;
```

Essentially, we are setting the loop back by one digit, such that when the loop plays through it will miss the last author and thus not print it out with the additional comma and space:

```
if ($authors[$a2]) {
echo $authors[$a2];
print ', ';
}
}
```

So for each author except the last author in the array, the script is printing it out and following it with `', '` (a comma and a space). Now we just need to print out the last author by itself:

```
echo $authors[$lcount];
}
```

To test the script to this point, put a closing paragraph tag in here and a closing curly bracket. You can delete it or comment it out once we continue with the script.

```
print '</p>';
}
```

Also, change your query to "handbook of health psychology." This book contains more than two authors and thus is a good test item to see how things are working. You should see the cover image and the title, followed by the authors listed with a comma and space after each except for the last author.

What you won't see, however, are those books that have only one author. We need to account for that possibility as well. So delete the previous line where you print out a closing paragraph tag and continue with our logic:

```
elseif ($acount = 1) {
```

This is related to the first `if` statement, which checks to see if `$acount` is greater than one. This line is saying that if that is not true and also if `$acount` equals one, then do the following:

```
for ($j = 0; $j < $acount; $j++) {
echo $authors[$j];
}
```

This is straightforward. Since there is only one author, all that we need to do is print the text out and not worry about commas or spaces or anything. Now close out this bit:

```
}
print '</p>';
```

We are now finished with the author segment of this script. All that remains to be displayed is the short description each book has and any links to downloadable content. First, let's print out the description. This is fairly simple:

```
print '<p>' . $data->items[$i]->volumeInfo->description . '</p>';
```

Next, we will print out links to downloadable content such as an ePub or PDF of the book. Since the Google Books API offers these two file types as the only options, we can include some simple if logic to print out the respective links:

```
if ($data->items[$i]->accessInfo->epub) {
print '<br />';
print '<a href="' . $data->items[$i]->accessInfo->epub->downloadLink .
    '">Download ePub Now</a>';
}
```

This if logic is saying that if there is an epub field in the array then print out the corresponding URL as a hyperlink. Same with the following statement, which is checking for a PDF:

```
if ($data->items[$i]->accessInfo->pdf) {
print '<br />';
print '<a href="' . $data->items[$i]->accessInfo->pdf->downloadLink .
    '">Download PDF Now</a>';
}
```

Finally, we will print out the preview link for each book in the array and close out the encompassing for loop and end the PHP script:

```
print '<br />';
print '<a href="' . $data->items[$i]->volumeInfo->previewLink . '">View
    Preview</a>';
print '<br />';
}
?>
```

Handbook of health psychology and aging

Carolyn M. Aldwin, Crystal L. Park, Avron Spiro

Offering a fresh, authoritative take on a topic of increasing relevance, this book is compr related fields pool their knowledge.

Download ePub Now
Download PDF Now
View Preview

Here's the complete script:

```php
<?php
$k = "your_key_here";
$q = urlencode("handbook of health psychology");
$url = "https://www.googleapis.com/books/v1/volumes?q=";
$url .= "$q";
$url .= "&key=$k";
$raw_data = file_get_contents($url);
$data = json_decode($raw_data);
$count = count($data->items);
for ($i = 0; $i < $count; $i++) {
print '<img src="' . $data->items[$i]->volumeInfo->imageLinks->thumbnail . '"
        />';
print '<h2>' . $data->items[$i]->volumeInfo->title . '</h2>';
$authors = $data->items[$i]->volumeInfo->authors;
$acount = count($authors);
$lcount = ($acount-1);
print '<p>';
if ($acount > 1) {
for ($j = 0; $j < $acount; $j++) {
$a2 = $j-1;
if ($authors[$a2]){
echo $authors[$a2];
print ', ';
}
}
echo $authors[$lcount];
}
elseif ($acount = 1) {
for ($j = 0; $j < $acount; $j++) {
```

```php
  echo $authors[$j];
  }
  }
print '</p>';
print '<p>' . $data->items[$i]->volumeInfo->description . '</p>';
if ($data->items[$i]->accessInfo->epub) {
print '<br />';
print '<a href="' . $data->items[$i]->accessInfo->epub->downloadLink .
    '">Download ePub Now</a>';
}
if ($data->items[$i]->accessInfo->pdf) {
print '<br />';
print '<a href="' . $data->items[$i]->accessInfo->pdf->downloadLink .
    '">Download PDF Now</a>';
}
print '<br />';
print '<a href="' . $data->items[$i]->volumeInfo->previewLink . '">View
    Preview</a>';
print '<br />';
}
?>
```